the Recovering People Pleaser

READER BONUS!

Because you are embarking on the courageous journey of self-discovery, healing and reclaiming your personal power, we're extending an exclusive offer to the readers of

The Recovering People Pleaser

We want to help jumpstart your process by offering you **three guided self-love meditations**, written and recorded by Kristen Brown.

Whether you are new to meditation or a pro, these guided meditations will help you replace self-doubt and unworthiness with self-value and confidence to foster a more empowered state of being.

Cheers to you, beloved soul sibling! For those who dedicate themselves to this sacred work, success is certain!

This special bonus is available for a limited time.

Sign up to receive your FREE meditations today!

For those unfamiliar with QR codes, simply open the camera app on your mobile device, hover over the QR code, and tap the link.

Peace and Love,

Kristen Brown

the Recovering People Pleaser

——— **A Spiritual Guide** ———
to Reclaim Your True Worth
and Attract the Love You Deserve

KRISTEN BROWN

Email: hello@kristenbrown.org

Website: www.kristenbrown.org

ISBN # (paperback) 979-8-218-06077-0

ISBN # (Kindle) 979-8-218-06078-7

Published by Action Takers Publishing™

Praise for Kristen Brown and
The Recovering People Pleaser

Kristen Brown is a gifted author and teacher who is incredibly real and relatable. I started reading *The Recovering People Pleaser* and I couldn't put it down! It is by far the best material I've read on this topic. This book is elegantly written to keep giving every time you read it. Huge kudos to Kristen for her masterful work!

-R.T., Law Professor

The Recovering People Pleaser is a beautiful guidebook for taking back your true power in any relationship! Kristen Brown generously pours her heart, soul, and direct experience into this richly filled book of insight on self-empowerment. Readers will take away priceless nuggets of wisdom on how to live from a more liberating, creative, and free state of mind with anyone in their life.

- Howard Falco, Spiritual Teacher, and the Author of I AM: The Power of Discovering Who You Really Are

If there is only one book to read that will change your life, it should be this one. If you suffer from people pleasing you are holding the key that will set you free. Written with heart, wisdom and grace, Kristen Brown will give you the tools and tough love you need to transform all your relationships.

-Andy Dooley, Law of Attraction Expert and Creator of the Manifestor's Café

As a recovering People Pleaser, I was anxiously awaiting the release of Kristen Brown's new book *The Recovering People Pleaser*. And boy, does Kristen deliver a power punch of a message about how to attract the love we all deserve. Her raw and personal accounts of growing up a People Pleaser will help millions of human beings stop living their lives for others and start living and creating their own unique lives, filled with joy and love. I highly recommend this book to anyone who just can't quite figure out why they've not yet attracted the love and the people they're longing for. Two thumbs up, 5 stars, and a top rating on any other rating scale as far as I am concerned!

-Roman Wyden, Host of ADHD IS OVER Podcast

Rarely do you come across a book that can truly rebuild your life (from the inside out) in such actionable ways. Kristen Brown has a way of explaining the complex in beautifully simple and memorable language. After reading this book, you will see your life with more clarity and feel vastly more empowered!

-Daryl Ledyard, Host of Deeper Planet Podcast

There are many (so-called) experts in the field of self-love, personal development, and relationship healing. However, there's no one with the compassion, empathy, wisdom, understanding, grace, and down-to-earth presence as Kristen Brown. Hearing her speak, and reading her words, makes you feel like she knows exactly how it feels to struggle through life and difficult relationships to come out on the other side a more whole, blessed, and fulfilled person. It's easy to consider her a friend and ally in this journey we're on in self-discovery. Having the honor of being her friend, I've gotten to witness and experience her incredible transformation superpowers in countless people's lives. This book provides the playbook to truly take your life, your heart, and your relationships to amazing and beautiful places where Love isn't a fantasy. It's a reality that's better than you could ask for or imagine.

-D Grant Smith, The Relationship Growth Farmer and author of Be Solid: How To Go Through Hell & Come Out Whole

I have always strived to be the "best" person possible. In essence, I had all of my "ducks in a row", except in my intimate relationships. Unfortunately, my search over the years for the "formula" to find true happiness never came until I found my spiritual coach, Kristen Brown! She is the "real deal" as her experiences, knowledge, and bright light have led me on my spiritual path which involves self-love, respect, and personal empowerment, and I have not looked back!

-Kristi Sparks, Retired College and Elementary Educator with Masters Degrees in Educational Leadership and Reading

Two years ago I was in the middle of another messy and painful breakup. Kristen Brown helped me understand why my low self-confidence was a homing beacon for the types of men I attracted. Session after session, with patience, kindness, grace, and humor, she guided me on a spiritual journey of exploration and healing. *The Recovering People Pleaser* is a gold mine of the brilliant wisdom and insight that Kristen embodies. It is a wake-up call and must-read for those of us committed to the magical path of personal empowerment and soul growth.

−Heather Eberle, Writer and Copy Editor

When I received a life-transforming epiphany, which I like to call "divine downloads," I immediately knew exactly who I NEEDED to talk it through with me. The one, the only, Kristen Brown! Having listened to Kristen share her LIVE "Top Mentor" thoughts on a social audio app, and having conversed with her regularly, I had ZERO doubts that she would listen intently with her heart, ask clarifying questions, share her own journey openly, and provide profoundly helpful and loving feedback/ input/insight/clarity to my own journey. I have the utmost respect and admiration for her heart, wisdom, and intention. I am truly honored and overjoyed to call her my friend and celebrate her amazing book that captures and expresses her transformative words — and the music behind those words, which is a soundtrack of empathy, compassion, and unconditional love. Read it and weep tears of love, peace, and JOY!

−Joseph "MoJOE" McCarthy, Professional Speaker, Podcaster, Author, and Leadership Development Consultant

Contents

Preface: **From My Heart to Yours**   xiii

Part One:

Where People Pleasing Comes From—Understanding the Origin

ONE: **Relationships are Mirrors**... 3

The Worthiness Cup   11

It's an Inside Job   16

Awareness is Key   17

Shifting Perceptions   19

TWO: **Energy—Your Vibe Don't Lie**................................. 23

The Magic of Raising Your Vibration   27

Different Places on Our Journeys   31

The Fear of Not Being Liked   34

Part Two:

Resetting the Foundation—Let the Healing Begin!

THREE: **Retraining Your Brain**.. 39

Fierceness is Required   43

Reframing Limiting Beliefs   46

FOUR: **The Emotional Guidance System**......................... 55

Why Repression Works Against Us   58

What Emotions Are and Are Not   60

Listening to Your Body   61

Emotions are Energy   64

FIVE: **Taking Radical Responsibility for Your Life**.......71

Owning Your Part   76

Own Only What's Yours   80

Discovering Our Unconscious Wounds   81

Emotional Triggers   85

How Triggers are Created   88

Healing Trauma Triggers   89

SIX: **The Miracle Cure** 95

The Most Important Relationship   97

Our Intrinsic vs. Extrinsic Value   99

Love is the Answer   101

SEVEN: **Setting Healthy Boundaries** 133

What are Boundaries?   134

Which Comes First—Self-Love or Boundaries?   137

Boundaries Serve Both People   139

Action Boundaries—When Words Aren't Working   142

Speak Up Sooner   145

Giving Grace to the Boundary Receiver   148

Boundaries in Hindsight   153

The Two Biggest Boundary Mistakes   155

EIGHT: **Connect with Your Divinity** 159

Calming the Nervous System   161

Contents

Intuition—Connecting with Your Inner Guidance 165

The Magic of Surrender 170

Forgiveness of Others 173

The Universe is Abundant 180

♡ From My Heart to Yours ♡

Dearest Reader,

I don't believe in coincidences. I believe all things in life are divine and purposeful and you were guided here for a reason. I commend you for following your inner guidance and for being the courageous Truth seeker that you are, *for those who seek will eventually find.*

The fact that you chose this book tells me you're moving away from the influences of your past and closer to an empowered future. I also suspect you are a sacred rebel—a person who is no longer willing to settle for the status quo or the conditions you've been living under. Something deep inside is beckoning you to explore, discover, and experience an improved reality. Although you may not realize it yet, you are joined by multitudes of others who are ready to release the dictates of their past to reclaim their personal power. We are an energetic tribe.

The Recovering People Pleaser is a conglomeration of my personal experiences and healing journey interwoven with principles that I call capital "T" truth. Truth that is of the highest, most intelligent energy. Truth that is ever-present and never changing. Truth that is of the highest essence of Love. I call this Truth by many names: God, Source, Universe, Higher Power, Source Energy, and Divine Intelligence just to name a few. I alternate these names throughout this book as directed by my inner creative guide. Regardless of which name I use, understand it refers to the Superpower of the Universe that is nothing other than the essence of Pure Love energy.

I understand that many of you have experienced what is commonly referred to as "religious trauma," and some spiritual nomenclature may feel triggering. I, too, have experienced the effects of fear-based religion and I completely understand. I assure you, this book was not written from the doctrine of any organized religion, nor does it contain any fear-based dogma that you'll need to wade through. I invite and encourage you to replace any language that feels resistant or triggering with something that feels more comfortable. From this point forward *you* get to decide what feels right, true, and acceptable for you.

I also invite you to read the words within these pages with an open heart and mind. Give yourself permission to adopt the best and leave the rest. I would never be so bold as to assume where you're at on your journey or what the ideal path to your healing will be. I'm just a girl in the world sharing my experience and wisdom in hopes of inspiring and motivating others to stop accepting the unacceptable and claim a future brimming with Real Love connections!

With the abundance of information and media that is available to us all, I do not take for granted that you chose to purchase my book. Yet, it doesn't surprise me because I wrote this book for you. Every chapter, every paragraph, and every word are infused with pure love and intention to beckon to those who will benefit from it.

Graciously, humbly, and with so much love, your soul sister,

A queen is wise. She has earned her serenity, not having had it bestowed on her but having passed her tests. She has suffered and grown more beautiful because of it. She has proved she can hold her kingdom together. She has become its vision. She cares deeply about something bigger than herself. She rules with authentic power.

~ Marianne Williamson, author of A Return to Love

Part One

Where People Pleasing Comes From – Understanding the Origin

Chapter One

Relationships are Mirrors

Relationship is a mirror to see yourself. Not as you would wish to be, but as you are.

~Jiddu Krishnamurti

I see you, soul sibling. You're kind, loving, and loyal. You're an earth angel, a lover, and a giver. You're intelligent and successful in most areas of your life, with the exception of romantic and/or personal relationships. It hurts you to watch people hurt and you'd do anything to never hurt another person. Your greatest desire is to love and to be loved. You're likely the listening ear everyone calls for help and are willing to drop what you're doing when someone needs you. If you investigate deeper, you may have been a "rescuer" in some (if not all) of your relationships. You're likely empathic and there's a good chance you're an HSP (Highly Sensitive Person). You feel others' pain and are quick to form deep connections.

You have no problem attracting friends and partners, yet some don't return the loyalty and love you give to them. They seem to take more than they give. You feel taken for granted, undervalued, and unappreciated. In some cases, you've been mentally, emotionally, or physically used, abused, or abandoned. You're confused why your loving heart rarely receives the nurturing it craves.

If you speak up about your feelings, you're likely met with defense, lack of ownership, gaslighting, or abandonment. Or you're told they'll do better by you, but nothing changes. You've lost yourself in most of your relationships and have become a shell of who you once were. You say love or loyalty keeps you in the relationship, but you're not sure that's true anymore. It almost feels like an unexplainable, invisible force is holding you there even though logic tells you something is not right.

I see you, beloved soul sibling, because I was you.

After decades of painful and lopsided relationships, I experienced the Mack Daddy of betrayals I refer to as "My Tsunami." Everything I'd spent a lifetime building that made me feel safe and secure in the world was destroyed through the reckless and selfish behavior of my second husband. In one of our last conversations, in an attempt to deflect from his behavior, he said, "You're going to have two divorces now! You're the common denominator!" I blew it off as the rantings of a narcissist.

Pfft. Whatever. We all know who the asshole is here (insert eye roll). Little did I know how profound those words would come to be.

Approximately a year and a half later, his words popped into my mind at a random time. I remember standing at the foot of my bed looking out the window while pondering them. He was not wrong. I *was* the common denominator in my past relationships. How could I not be? I was there for all of them. There was no denying I was the one constant variable. I also noticed my theme of attracting partners who didn't respect, protect, and cherish me. (This pattern was present in my friendships too.) In the past, I remember thinking I must have terrible luck, but it didn't keep me from trying again. I figured finding a good partner was a numbers game or the luck of the draw and if I kept pulling from the deck, I'd end up with a king eventually. But no matter how many times I tried, it never happened. I pulled one joker after the next. I began to see there was more to attracting quality people than luck. Somehow, *I* was contributing to this pattern of painful and lopsided relationships, but I didn't know how... yet.

It would've been easy to remain the victim and continue blaming them all. I'm certain if I'd taken my stories before a judge and jury, they'd all be guilty as charged. No morally sound person would ever think their behaviors were okay. And my ego would've loved it. But what's meant to grow us in life doesn't come by taking the easy road or the path of blame.

**Growth requires taking personal responsibility
for our piece of the equation.**

5

I didn't attract my past experiences through bad luck or some karmic repayment plan. There was something about me. *I* had attracted those types of partners and *I* needed to figure out how not to. I found it ironic and somewhat comical that the words meant to hurt me were the words that blessed me. They became the catalysts that led to healing my people pleasing pattern and embarking on an inspired mission to help others like me. I am forever grateful for those five words: *You are the common denominator.*

I was.

I am.

And you are too.

The moment I owned that reality, something cracked open inside me, and a ray of light entered. It felt freeing somehow, so I investigated further. I looked back on my entire romantic history from my first relationship at fifteen years old to the present day. I took inventory of how I was treated in each one and saw a common theme. Although some relationships were worse than others, in general I was disrespected, dishonored, taken for granted, and unprotected. My relationships were completely lopsided. I was doing all the giving while my partners were doing all the taking. Also, each romantic partner demonstrated some iteration of cheating, substance abuse, porn/sex addiction, and emotional or physical abuse.

I then heard a still, gentle voice I've come to understand as the voice of God ask me, *Now, how have you treated yourself in the same ways others have treated you?* Without stopping to wonder where the question came from, I responded with the following:

I disrespected myself by agreeing to sex before I was ready. I disrespected myself by doing things I didn't want to do. I disrespected myself when I chased after guys who had lost interest. I disrespected myself when I took partners back with little or no apologies and no real changes in behavior.

I didn't protect myself by staying with partners who verbally, emotionally, or physically abused me. I didn't protect myself when I agreed to things that were unsafe for my physical or emotional well-being. I didn't protect myself when I didn't maintain healthy boundaries.

I dishonored myself by putting others' needs and wants above my own. I dishonored myself by saying yes when my heart, intuition or logic was saying no. I dishonored myself by allowing myself to be used or taken for granted. I dishonored myself by staying with partners who betrayed me.

I didn't value myself by focusing on what I perceived was wrong with me rather than what was right with me. I didn't value myself by using negative words when speaking to and about myself. I didn't value myself by believing my body and looks were my only asset.

I took myself for granted by not appreciating my intelligence, wisdom, intuition, and morally sound person I am. I took myself for granted by not owning my greatness and stepping into it fully.

There it was, as clear as the sun hovering above me in the bright light of day. **My relationships mirrored how I treated myself.** Surprisingly, this knowledge didn't lead to feelings of sadness, anger, or shame. It felt good. It felt right and expansive. It felt peaceful. I've come to know that peace always comes when we open our hearts to Truth, when we finally clear away the grime that's been clouding our perceptions. My conversation with God continued...

God: Would you be your best friend?

Me: Heck yes, I'd be my best friend!

God: Why?

Me: Because I'm kind, loyal, generous, loving, giving, attentive, affectionate, smart, honest, hardworking... and the list went on.

God: Then why are you allowing people to treat you any less than that?

Me: ...

Why *was* I allowing it? Why *couldn't* I stand in my power? Why *did* I keep attracting the same bullshit over and over again? I had no idea. All I knew was I couldn't stand to be in another lopsided relationship. I needed to figure out how to attract a partner whose love and respect were equal to mine. In that sacred moment, I vowed to remain single and celibate until I figured out what was causing the pattern and how to break free of it for good.

#TimeFrameUndetermined

I didn't know how long it would take or what it would involve, but I didn't care. Even if it meant I'd be single forever, it would be an improvement from what I had endured.

I was so dedicated that I didn't so much as have a cup of coffee with a single man. Enough was enough. Something wasn't right and I was driven to figure it out. The only thing I knew for sure was I would not attempt another relationship until I felt something had changed. I trusted

I'd know when that something occurred, and I gave my healing to my Higher Power. I filled my eyes, ears, and mind with only high vibrational literature and media. I talked to God, meditated, and journaled. My healing became one of my top priorities. I turned my alone time into re-creation time. I refer to that era in my life as *The College of Kristen* because it was a period of concentrated focus, learning, and dedication, much like earning a college degree. It was the best thing I ever did for myself and the reason I wrote this book.

After a while, I noticed subtle changes in the way I viewed life, how I was handling situations and how willing I was to respect and protect myself. The old me was giving way and a new me was emerging. It was incredible. I couldn't tell you exactly when this happened during my *College of Kristen* because I wasn't keeping track. My best guess is that it took somewhere around a year. Not only did I *feel* different, but my behavior started reflecting this new foundation.

One day, the guy I dated for a short time after my second divorce (full story in an upcoming chapter) texted me. The old me would've overthought my response and had a covert motive to keep his attention or try to get him to see me. This time was different. Without any preemptive thoughts, motives, or hesitation, I glanced at my phone and thought, *Eh, I don't need to respond to that.* No judgment, no drama, no anything—I was completely unattached. I was walking into my mother's house when this happened, and I stopped dead in my tracks. *What—the fuck—was that? No, seriously. That was so unlike me. What just happened here?*

As I stood motionless in my mother's foyer, it dawned on me that something was changing inside me. My dedication was paying off. I asked myself what had changed. Where was this new behavior coming from? I realized for the first time that it came from my newfound sense of self-worth. This was the moment I understood for the very first time that hidden unworthiness had been running the show for the majority of my life. But worthiness was running it now.

Over-giving and over-accommodating Kristen had vanished and was replaced with worthy, valuable, and centered Kristen. I also realized this alteration didn't happen through force. Rather, it was a gentle evolution I'd become available to by letting go (of control and outcome) and focusing only on my healing. A subtle, yet powerful, transformation was shining through.

All real change happens on the inside first, which
***naturally* shifts the way we think and act.**

We don't have to force, manipulate, or strategize to create healthy relationships. Instead, we heal our wounded places and then follow the guidance that comes from our new energetic space.

Then I did the next thing my heart guided me to do. I wrapped my arms around my body and gave myself a big, warm hug. I praised myself like a small child who'd learned a new skill. *Look at you! You're doing so great, Kristen! Wow! Did you see that? You're healing!* To this day, I hug myself and pat myself on the back for any empowered move I make, no matter how insignificant it might seem. I encourage you to do the same, even if you feel ridiculous doing so. Those two simple actions, combined with the wisdom and practices in this book, will profoundly alter the place inside you responsible for the level of empowerment you show to the world. Here's why.

The Worthiness Cup

To be beautiful means to be yourself. You don't need to be accepted by others. You need to accept yourself.

~ Thich Nhat Hanh

I want you to imagine a medium-sized plastic drinking cup situated in the center of your chest over your heart. The cup is open at the top and has a hinged bottom where it can swing open but stay attached. You can make it any color or style you choose. Mine looks like a simple plastic tumbler that is reddish-colored. This is your worthiness cup. We all have one and it's where our self-worth is stored.

Our level of self-worth is directly proportional to the quality of treatment we require from others.

When our cups are full, we're aligned with our true worth and we're not afraid to respect and protect ourselves above all else. This sends a message to the world that we are valuable. However, when our cups are low or empty, we become needy and desperate for love, approval, and attention. We're willing to compromise our sacred selves to feel (if even for a moment) that we matter. We believe that since our authentic selves didn't get us what we wanted in childhood, we must become someone else. We replace our True Selves with false identities (masks) designed to please others to feel safe. We dim our lights, play small, overanalyze, over-give, over-accommodate, over-think, give in, give up, and give over. We become fragmented versions of our authentic selves in hopes of filling this painful void inside.

> **The problem is that we cannot be loved for *who***
> ***we truly are* if we're presenting a false front.**

And somewhere deep inside we'll always question other people's love because we'll know they didn't fall in love with who we truly are.

You might be wondering if our worthiness cups were once full, how did they get empty? What I share in the following sections is *integral* to understanding how the worthiness cup works and what we can do to refill it and keep it full. This awareness is *essential* for breaking free from our disempowered relationship patterns forever. In the next two sections, I explain the cup from two perspectives, the spiritual and the physiological, with the hope of providing a greater understanding.

The Worthiness Cup—The Spiritual Perspective

When our souls enter our physical bodies at birth, we know nothing other than where we came from—the unconditional love of God/ Source/Universe. We know only that our divine essences and worthiness cups are full. We are connected to our authentic selves and are not concerned about the judgments of others. As we grow in our human bodies, we take in messages and experiences from the external world. These direct and indirect messages come via our parents, authority figures, friends, religions, traumas, media, and society. The messages are interpreted through our newly forming egos. They tell us we're too much, not enough, bad, bothersome, problematic, unimportant, and so forth.

The ego is the first and loudest voice in our heads, so we believe what it's saying. We form subconscious beliefs that support the ego's interpretation that there's something wrong or unlovable about us, and we must become something else to fit in, find acceptance, and receive love. This is how hidden shame and unworthiness take root, dropping the bottoms off our worthiness cups and allowing our self-worth to drain out. The result is that we feel desperate and needy to fill the painful void.

Note: Sometimes unworthiness develops into hidden desperation and neediness known as **hyper-dependence** (making *others'* needs one's primary focus). And sometimes it presents as **hyper-independence** (making one's *own* needs their primary focus), which may also include a lack of empathy and deep connections. We typically lean toward one side of the spectrum and there are also varying degrees of both behaviors, ranging from mild to extreme. Where you fall on the spectrum is not super important. The end goal is the same for both—to find an optimal position *between* the two polarities. This is referred to as **interdependence**—a healthy balance between tending to the needs of others while tending to the needs of self.

The Worthiness Cup—
The Scientific/Physiological Perspective

From birth to two years, our brains are in the lowest brain wave state called delta. In this state, we are mostly unconscious and fully connected to our inner worlds (Divine/Authentic Self). From two to six years, we enter a faster brain wave state called theta. This is a twilight, lucid state known as the subconscious. It's the brainwave state achieved with meditation. In theta, we're still connected to our inner worlds but we're starting to "wake up" to the outer world. From six to twelve years, we shift to a higher brain wave state called alpha. In this state, we become more aware of our environments. Our awareness begins to shift from our inner worlds to our outer worlds and we start to take in external information. This is when most of our "programming" occurs. Around age twelve, we move into the next state called beta, denoted by smaller, faster brainwaves. Beta is associated with mental, intellectual, and outward focus. In this state, our awareness turns to the outer world.

As we grow and evolve from unconscious to conscious, the ego starts to form. The ego is the part of our psyche designed to keep us safe. Its job is to scan and interpret our environments for potential threats, both emotional and physical. It then alerts us to these perceived threats through fear-based thoughts that often promote fear-based actions better known as "control."

During our physiological growth, the ego receives and processes *direct and indirect* messages about who we are. These messages may have been told to us, or they came via the ego's interpretation of both traumatic and non-traumatic experiences. The louder the ego gets, the less in tune we become with our inner worlds—God Self/Higher Self (our authentic self)—and the more in tune we become with our ego self/lower self (false self). Therefore, we begin to believe the outer world over the inner world. This is when false beliefs about ourselves and the world take form. These false beliefs become our programmed or auto-pilot ways of thinking and behaving and contribute to the "faulty" foundation we try to relationship from.

From both the spiritual and physiological perspectives, we unconsciously believe that since the outer world took away our worth, the outer world must be how we get it back. We're driven by an unconscious mechanism that says, *I need to get from the outside what is missing on the inside.* Our focus swivels away from our True Selves toward becoming who *we think* others want us to be to gain love, approval, and acceptance. Enter: The People Pleaser.

Merriam Webster's dictionary describes a People Pleaser as *a person who has an emotional need to please others often **at the expense of** his or her own needs or desires.* The keywords to focus on here are, "at the expense of." People Pleasers are known to over-give and over-accommodate and have little to no guidelines, limits, or personal boundaries with others, at the expense of themselves. They're also quite adept at becoming who they think others want them to be.

Here's the clincher. Remember when I described you/me at the beginning of this chapter as lovers, givers, and Earth angels? This is entirely true. We're gentle, kind, and giving *by nature.* The desire to help and give to others comes naturally to us. Because a People Pleaser's genuine nature is loving, it can be confusing and difficult to discern where to draw the line in relationships. Allow me to break it down a little further.

Being a giver is not the problem. It's OVER giving that is.

Being accommodating is not the problem. It's OVER accommodating that is.

Being understanding is not the problem. It's OVER understanding that is.

**Anytime we give at the expense of our well-being
means we're unconsciously looking for love
and approval outside ourselves.**

And if we're really honest, people pleasing is a form of control. We're covertly attempting to control how others view us.

At each given moment, our actions are either stemming from our God Selves or our ego selves. There is no in-between. We're either in alignment with Love or we're in alignment with fear. This concept makes it easier for me to check my feelings and motives regarding the choices and decisions I make in relationships. I ask myself: *Am I deciding from a place of fear and control or am I deciding from a place of self-worth and detachment?* By slowing down our thought processes and consulting our motives, we're likely to make much better decisions for ourselves.

It's an Inside Job

Change the person in the mirror and your world will change.

~ Rhonda Byrne

Have you ever noticed when you receive a compliment or some type of approval or attention it feels good in the moment, but the feeling doesn't last long? That's because outside approval and acceptance don't stick. They are not the cures to filling our worthiness cups. Unworthiness is always on the lookout for its next hit of approval so we can survive another week, another day, another hour. I liken it to an insatiable beast forever scanning for its next source of sustenance. And much like drug addicts are willing to forsake those they love to get their next hits, we forsake our sacred selves over and over again to get ours. But we're never fully satisfied. Here's why. *Outside* love, approval, and attention enter through the tops of our cups and fly out the bottoms. They don't stick because they are not the antidote. If it was that easy to fill our cups, we'd all be emotionally satiated and happy. Instead, our cups remain empty because we're attempting to fill them from *the wrong sources*.

The only remedy for filling our worthiness cups is **giving ourselves the unconditional love** we've been trying in vain to get from others. (Much more on this in an upcoming chapter.)

Awareness is Key

> *Awareness is like the sun. When it shines on*
> *things they are transformed.*
>
> ~ Thich Nhat Hanh

The fact that you're reading this book tells me you're recognizing a pattern in your life and you're likely sick and tired of being sick and tired. You're seeking solutions, which also tells me you're open to new ideas to create a better life experience. Let's pause a moment while I congratulate you! You have entered the healing path! I know it's been a long and tiresome journey, but you're here now and I couldn't be happier for you! You might feel like you had no choice because it was rough out there, but we all have choices. It's called free will. Free will affords us the freedom to make choices and decisions along our paths and you've chosen to become your own hero! Fist bump! Hip bump! And high ten to you!

You might think that's a bit of an overreaction for simply reading a book. But here's what I know for sure: **people who seek will eventually find.** The path to empowerment and attracting and creating healthy relationships *requires* gathering new information, a willingness to shift perceptions, and honest self-observation and self-inquiry.

We cannot heal that which we are unaware of.

Therefore, awareness is key! The better you get to know yourself, the faster you will heal. To take it another step forward, I invite you to process all you're reading in this book with an open heart and mind. Resist the ego's urge to deny what is trying to come to light. Denial is the ego's way of keeping you from becoming aware because your awareness will lead to its death. The ego is cunning and a master at deception. Its only concern is to preserve itself. It does this by keeping us from Truth. However, don't try to make something fit that doesn't fit for you. Reclaiming your power requires trusting yourself and your inner knowing above anything or anyone else.

Additionally, do your best to refrain from judging or criticizing yourself for where you've been. Self-criticism and judgment are the ego's life force. The lower you are, the "happier" ego is. Judgment and shame keep your worthiness cup empty and will only perpetuate your pattern. Remember the words of the beloved Maya Angelou, "When you know better, you do better." We are all doing the best we can at any given moment. If we had known better, we would have done better. Give yourself the same grace you'd give a baby learning to feed themselves or a toddler learning to walk. Would you shame a baby for missing their mouth with a spoonful of mashed carrots? Would you shame a crawling toddler for not running as soon as they stood up? No, you wouldn't. You'd celebrate each little victory! It's time to turn your compassion and kindness inward. Give to yourself what you've always given to others.

We face consistent challenges on this spiritual journey. We're not supposed to know everything in advance—we wouldn't be here if we did. Our souls chose to have this experience to grow. To shame ourselves for things we knew nothing about is ludicrous and will not serve our healing paths. From here forward practice grace, forgiveness, and compassion for yourself. Filling your worthiness cup starts now.

Shifting Perceptions

It's not what happens to you that is as crucial as it is how you perceive it and what you decide to do with or without it.

~ Dr. John Demartini

Studies show that humans think 60,000-70,000 thoughts a day and 90% of those thoughts repeat from one day to the next.

Repeating thoughts create beliefs and repeating beliefs create our realities.

So, it's fair to say the realities we experience stem from our levels of thinking. Unless or until we change these levels of thinking and believing, we'll keep our autopilots engaged and continue to get the same results. It is unreasonable to expect an improved experience when we're thinking the same thoughts, believing the same beliefs, and acting from the same foundation. To change our realities, we must be willing to change our thoughts.

We do this by opening our hearts and minds to what I call capital "T" Truth. Truth that is from the highest level of consciousness. Truth that is indisputable and infinite. Truth that is unchanging and can redirect your life in the highest possible way. When we're aware, we'll recognize this Truth by its resonance or what I call "ringing true." It has a peaceful and expansive essence about it because it's derived from the highest possible energy. It's the energy of God/Source/Universe—the energy of Love. When you read or hear something that rings true, make it your new truth. Don't hesitate, don't delay, don't question it to death. Adopt it. Journal about it. Marinate on it and absorb it.

Often when we're stuck in a pattern, we hear or read something wise, but skip over it because we don't think one little idea can have a significant impact. On the contrary! One shift in perception can send a shock wave into the Universe for more like it to come. Can you imagine what many small shifts in perception can do?! By absorbing Truth, you will begin to heal from a foundational level—the level of the mind. And because your outer world always reflects your inner world, as you heal your mind, your life and experiences will improve.

At our core, human beings want to feel safe and comfortable. It might feel "easier" to stay with what's familiar because we know what to expect. But this familiarity we're clinging to has not served our highest good. It's part of the cyclical thinking and believing that has perpetuated our pattern.

**Healing work requires getting comfortable
with being uncomfortable.**

Learning to love yourself and filling your worthiness cup is not what I'd describe as difficult or scary—it's simply different. It's about understanding that our old methods of operating aren't working and adopting new methods that will. However, the "uncomfortable" will never be something that would hurt you or another person.

**Universal Truth always works for the highest
good of all concerned.**

It may feel awkward at first because you're used to your old way of living. Try looking at it like this. Imagine if you were offered a million dollars to walk a mile with a tiny pebble in your shoe. The pebble is too small to cause damage, but it's somewhat uncomfortable to walk with. Knowing there's a huge payoff at the end, would you accept a little discomfort to get there? For most people, the answer would be yes. Every great payoff in life happens right outside our comfort zones. The healing path entails stepping away from what's familiar and has perpetuated your story to having the courage to try something new.

**The time has come to unlearn what no longer
serves you and replace it with what will.**

Each of us has different upbringings, experiences, traumas, cultures, and spiritual views that culminate into who we are. Although we classify as "People Pleasers," we're on a spectrum. Your level of pleasing does not determine how "broken" you are or how long your healing will take. Healing is personal to everyone. That said, I've seen that people on a mission to heal will do so faster. This happens when their hearts are open, their minds are receptive, and they make continued efforts with intentional focus.

Give yourself permission to share what you're learning or keep it to yourself. Your healing is not dependent on who knows what you're working on. This is an inside job between you and God. Be mindful during this time to only consume information from people, influencers, authors, and mentors who are love-based and want to see you win! Anything that uplifts, inspires, or motivates you is a heck YES! Anything that demeans you or makes you feel poor is a heck NO! Universal Truth will never feel bad; it will always feel uplifting. Self-honoring begins by setting clear limits for yourself and following through with self-discipline. If something doesn't contribute to raising your vibe, it's out! This is the first step to popping the bottom back on your worthiness cup and filling it up!

Chapter Two

Energy—Your Vibe Don't Lie

Everything is energy and that's all there is to it. Match the frequency of the reality you want, and you cannot help but get that reality. It can be no other way. This is not philosophy. This is physics.

~ Bashar

Everything is energy. The landscape you see, the chair you're sitting on, the food you eat, and the people around you. The world is made of energy. This is called The Law of Vibration. All matter vibrates at a certain frequency, including people. It's known in quantum physics that energetic frequencies attract like frequencies. This is called The Law of Attraction. Through my life experience and studies, I've learned quite a bit about energy and vibrational frequencies, which helped me understand relationship patterns on a whole new level. Each of us has what I call an "attractor factor." Our attractor factor determines "who" and "what" we draw to ourselves.

It's fair and logical to say that our energy attracts people and experiences to us. We don't attract low vibe or toxic people to us by sheer luck, nor is it a generational curse. It's our energetic vibrations that attract them. If we resonate with a frequency of "not valuable," we attract people who don't treat us as valuable. If we resonate with the energy of "I don't matter," we attract people who treat us like we don't matter. The opposite is also true. When you heal your inner world to reclaim your value and importance, you'll attract people who treat you the same.

You may be wondering how kind and gentle you attracted a narcissist, user, or abuser. Some people refer to this as the Empath-Narcissist Dynamic or they see it as darkness being attracted to the light. First off, we're all empaths. Every single one of us. We all have the ability to sense and feel energy, though some people are more in tune with this energy than others. Second, not all people who hurt us are narcissists. It's foolish to throw everyone into one of two categories, as there are far too many variables involved.

What is for sure, is that we are all the walking wounded. Each of us has experienced painful, traumatic, and dramatic experiences that have hurt us in some capacity. And we all carry shame and unworthiness because of it.

**Shame and unworthiness are the true
plagues on this planet.**

For some people, shame and unworthiness present as people pleasing, hyper-dependence, and neediness. For others, they present as selfishness, hyper-independence, and guardedness. Neither presentation is better than the other. They're simply two opposing ways our wounds dictate our behaviors. Additionally, there are levels or degrees of both behaviors, and they can range from mild to extreme. Therefore, a mild People Pleaser will likely attract a mild narcissist. An extreme People Pleaser will likely attract an extreme narcissist. It's unlikely a mild People Pleaser would attract or stay with an extreme narcissist and vice versa.

What's important to understand is that People Pleasers and narcissists are vibrational matches to whatever level they're on. A narcissist or selfish person is looking for someone who will make everything about them. They are the takers. A People Pleaser is a person who makes it about everyone else. They are the givers. The behaviors are a vibrational match—they click like a key fitting a lock. Therefore, many of us over-givers have joined in relationships with over-takers. I refer to this as the Giver-Taker Dynamic.

Note: I don't believe all selfish people are narcissists. I believe some people have narcissistic tendencies and behaviors but would not have clinical diagnoses as such. Let's remember that Narcissistic Personality Disorder (NPD) is a true personality disorder. Be mindful not to label someone simply because they're difficult to deal with. I used the term narcissist in the writing above because it's become a term pop culture easily identifies with when talking about a specific type of person/behavior. But from here forward, I'll be referring to them as Takers.

The ultimate goal of our healing work is to land somewhere between the two polarities to attract individuals in the same vibrational space or to bring healing to our existing relationships. The understandings you're coming to and the inner work you'll be doing via this book are designed to shift your energetic frequency to stop attracting people who are only interested in taking from you and/or to heal current dysfunctional dynamics. It can't not.

**When your inner world changes, your
outer world changes with it.**

No matter how our shame and unworthiness show up (over-giving or over-taking), the healing work is the same. What we heal on the inside will shift our experiences on the outside. As the legendary Hellenistic figure Hermes Trismegistus, once wrote, "As within, so without." Healing brings us closer to functioning between the two polarities—neither too giving nor too taking, but somewhere right in between.

The Magic of Raising Your Vibration

The higher you raise your vibration and frequency, the more
attractive you become personally and professionally.

~ Ken Lauher

The same way our outer world reflects our *lack* of self-worth, it will reflect our *abundance* of self-worth. As we're healing, we'll see this happen in a couple of ways. I call these "Wins," as they're indicators that we are treating ourselves better!

Win One—High vibe people repel low vibe people.

When we raise our vibrations (heal our shame and unworthiness), we'll *repel* people with lower vibrations. Yep, you read that correctly. By showing up in the world firmly rooted in our self-worth and unapologetically being who we are, we emit a higher energetic frequency. This repels people of lower frequencies because we're not aligned.

At first, it might appear as if they don't like you, or are snubbing you or ignoring you. It might feel startling because a People Pleaser's greatest desire is to win the approval of others. The old familiar panicky feeling of not being liked may resurface. You might be tempted to return to your old habits of pleasing, but they won't feel as alluring as they once were. Remember, repelling happens *after* you've raised your vibration. The new foundation (energetic frequency) you function from won't be as driven by fear as your old foundation was. Your lens will be clearer, and you'll start to see it for what it is—the other person is not a good match for you. You'll come to understand on a visceral level that their rejection is not only your protection, but also a positive sign your vibration is rising.

Over-takers are looking for easy prey. It's what David Buss, an evolutionary psychologist at the University of Texas, calls "the exploitability factor." They're looking for someone they can possess, control, and manipulate; someone who won't challenge them. Individuals who are eager to please don't require much in return, put themselves last, and are weak with personal boundaries. They are perfect matches for over-takers. Much like having a sixth sense, a Taker will know a Giver when they see/feel one. There's a certain energy and particular behaviors that Givers emit that draw Takers to them like magnets.

Opposingly, a person with high self-value, confidence, and a willingness to stand in their power will feel off-putting to a Taker. They may not know why, but even the most physically attractive person will repel them. Therefore, *pretending* to be confident and worthy to deter Takers never yields the results we hope for. "Fake it 'til you make it" won't work here because yo' vibe don't lie!

Win Two — They grow, or they go.

What happens if you already have a Taker in your life and you raise your vibration? Most of us on the healing path have already experienced this but may not have understood what was happening. First, let's look at what this is not. Have you ever grown apart from someone you were once close to? Life changes and geographical distances can contribute to spending less time with certain people, but the love and connection are still there. And when you reconnect, it feels like no time has passed. This type of growing apart is *not* energy-related, but typically distance and schedule related.

A *vibrational disconnection* is when you're connected to someone for a period of time (long or short-term, it doesn't matter) and they start to annoy you, turn you off, frustrate you, or drain you. It feels taxing to spend considerable time with them. You might find yourself distancing from them without knowing why. This is where the term "energy vampire" comes from. Because it can feel like they're sucking the life from you. The truth is, no one can take energy from us that we don't permit them to take. It's more likely we're lowering our vibrations to match theirs because the dissonance is uncomfortable or we're not staying grounded while we're around them.

I remember a time this became apparent to me. I noticed when a certain person was around, I started looking for negative things to talk about. It took me off guard because I'm typically positive and solution-oriented and like to focus on what's going right rather than what's going wrong. Here's what's even more uncanny: on the day I noticed my negativity, the other person wasn't even being negative. I had dimmed my light to be around them so many times in the past that my body remembered and started to dim automatically. It was fascinating to witness. I now check in with myself when they're around to see if I'm keeping my vibration steady or if I'm tempted to lower it.

You may also notice a change on the other person's part. They could be feeling the same way about you that you're feeling about them. Ironic, eh? They might start calling or texting less, begin distancing from you, or dropping you altogether. Many times when this happens, it scares us because we take it as rejection. Since they're familiar players in our lives, we're comfortable with them or we've become dependent on them in some way. Sometimes we try to force a reconnection by dimming down or playing small. Although it might work for a little while, it's unsustainable long-term because it takes a lot of effort and energy to hold yourself back. Eventually, your True Self will shine through. I liken it to holding two-pound weights in front of you with outstretched arms. At first, it feels like nothing, but over time it becomes unbearable. And who's the one suffering by expending precious energy to be who you are not? You are.

But what happens if we refuse to lower our vibrations, dim our lights, or play small with them? What if we stay rooted in our growth, truth, and authenticity? This is where it gets magical!

The person will either grow or they'll go.

I know that last statement might be terrifying, as we're conditioned to want people to stay. But remember, you're reading this book to heal your lopsided and painful relationship patterns. This requires allowing people who resent your light or refuse to grow to leave your life. Their exit is nothing to take personally **because it's not about you**. Low vibe people find it difficult to be around high vibe people because your light shines on their unhealed places. You're like a ray of sunshine beaming through the windows of an abandoned house, illuminating dust bunnies and cobwebs in the corners. In essence, they know you "see them," and don't like that they can't hide from you. Since they're not yet willing to heal and grow, *you become annoying or unattractive to them.*

High vibration people are attractive, and I'm not referring to external beauty. Those with lower vibrations may be secretly jealous of you as they notice how people are drawn to you. It can feel "painful" to be around you as it's *your* attention people want.

Low vibers may try to knock you off the pedestal they have you on by saying things like, but not limited to, *You think you're all that. You think you're perfect. You're crazy. You need therapy. You think you know everything.* Or worse, they'll say bad things about you behind your back in hopes of lowering others' high opinions of you. Their "attacks" are feeble attempts to make you bad or wrong, so they don't have to look at themselves. How open a person's heart and mind are to Truth and expansion determines if they'll grow or go. In other words, some people are ready and some people are not. Either way, it has nothing to do with you. By taking it personally, you're saying another person's spiritual journey is about you—but it can't be. Everyone's unique journey is only between themselves and God. We might be players in their game of life, but we are never responsible for what they choose for themselves.

Different Places on Our Journeys

The fact that we're all different is
one thing we have in common.

~ Justin Young

I've been an intuitive, Truth seeker, and researcher of human nature for as long as I can remember. My first memory of receiving inner guidance (intuition) was in first grade when a boy in my class was giving away his hamster. The teacher instructed us to get permission from our parents if we wanted to be in the drawing to win it. As soon as the words were out of her mouth, I intuitively *knew* I was going to win. And I did. (His name was Tweety, and he was a good little hammy.)

I also can see what my friend describes as, "behind the veil." This means I often see beyond the "superficial" when it comes to people's situations and into the hidden fear directing their life experiences. I can see how and why they are stuck and what needs to be addressed for optimal outcomes. I'm also adept at "reading" the dynamic between two people. These abilities showed up around high school and strengthened as I got older. Whether you call it intuition, psychic, or energy reading, it's real, always on point and I trust it completely.

There's a line in the song "Lay It On The Line" by the band Triumph that I resonate with on such a deep level, I had it scrawled across the whiteboard in my kitchen for a long time. It says, "I don't ask for much—the truth will do just fine." I've been known to say, "Tell me the truth because I can work with that. I can't work with a lie." Because I feel this way about the truth, I assumed everyone else did too. But that wasn't the case. When I lovingly shared my "knowings" with others, it pushed them away. I was befuddled why others rejected me when I was respectfully (and with the highest intention) trying to help. Heck man, I love the truth! Truth is the gateway to solutions and compromise. Truth is the first thing I look for. Without the truth how can we make sound choices and decisions? Why would someone not want the truth?!

It wasn't until I started to see a pattern with the people who shied away from the truth (forever the researcher here), that I realized not everyone is at the same place on their journeys. **People are only ready for what they are ready for.** Where they're at has nothing to do with me or my worth. The fact that others ignore, reject, or detach from us when we're trying to shine light on their dim situations, doesn't mean we've done something bad or wrong.

There are no good guys or bad guys here. We're all Spirit in human form connected by God and on our unique spiritual expeditions. We can't fault someone for not yet learning what we've learned or healing at a different rate. Nor should we judge them for being closed and fearful. Their path is not ours to judge. Often the stakes haven't gotten high enough for them to start asking powerful questions and becoming curious about better solutions. In other words, **the pain of staying the same has not yet outweighed the fear and discomfort of change.** Many people resist change until their suffering reaches an unmanageable level. And when or if that happens is God's business, not ours. Our job is to focus on our healing and energy, no one else's.

On a positive note, many people are willing to heal and grow into more expanded versions of themselves. And when couples, friends, and family *grow* together, they often *stay* together. We may not be on the exact wavelength at all times, but our frequencies are close enough that it's manageable. Sometimes people leapfrog in their development—one grows then the other one surpasses them and so forth. In other cases, one grows first and the other one "catches up," so to speak. At any rate, both parties are expanding, and the possibilities are endless because there's an equilibrium in the relationship that keeps things balanced.

If we raise our vibrations and our person grows too, we win! If we raise our vibrations and our person goes, we also win because we now have space available to fill with a higher frequency person. The universe abhors a vacuum and will seek to fill that void as soon as possible with someone who matches your new energetic level as long as you're open to it. That's pretty darn exciting if you ask me!

The Fear of Not Being Liked

If you just set out to be liked, you would be
prepared to compromise on anything at any time,
and you would achieve nothing.

~ Margaret Thatcher

As Pleasers, we are afraid of upsetting others, hurting someone's feelings, and not being liked. Most Pleasers are great at noticing subtle shifts in facial expressions, body language, and vocal tones that cue us into "who we need to be" to win the acceptance or approval of that person. Or so we think.

Can we really be liked by everyone? Is it even possible?

Think about your favorite actor, musician, or favorite song. Are they everyone else's favorite too? Has anyone ever said, "Omg, you like that actor? They bug the crap out of me." Or "Yuck, I hate that song. Why do you like it?" Ask ten people who their Hollywood crushes are, and you'll likely get ten different answers. We all have different tastes, ideas of beauty, and personality types we're attracted to. So, the answer is no. We cannot win over all the people all the time. So how about we take the pressure off and stop trying?

Not long ago, I heard this concept: One-third of the people will love you. One-third of the people will not like you. One-third of the people will not care either way. When I first heard this my lower self freaked out. Omg, what do you mean not everyone will like me?! Then my Higher Self kicked in and said, *Oh, thank God. What a relief! I don't have to bend and flex and mold myself to be liked by everyone because not everyone is going to like me anyway!* I felt immense freedom the day I learned this concept. Some people might not like me, but the ones who do will be legit.

I used to be someone who'd jump willy-nilly into any new friendship or relationship. *I'll be your friend! I'll be your girlfriend! I don't care how messed up you are. My love will help you!* If I liked the person, I'd jump in with both feet. I didn't wait to learn more about them, discover their character, or see if we'd be a good fit. Part of this was innocence on my part because I believed everyone matched my intentions. The other part was a desire to be liked and to have people around me. Let's be honest, People Pleasers typically don't struggle to make new friends. We're kind, available, attentive, rarely say no, and we give, give, give. This makes us likable, but also easy targets for Takers.

When we start to own our worth and authentic natures, our friendship pool might empty a little or a lot. It all depends on the growth-ability of those currently around us. Like I mentioned earlier, they'll either grow or they'll go. The good news is through self-healing we become less attached to who comes and who goes because (a.) we won't be needy and desperate (b.) we now understand how energy works and (c.) we're happy in our own company.

I understand that this energy concept may disrupt all you've thought to be true and may take a minute to sink in. However, I am certain that by the end of this book, you'll see your lopsided relationship patterns from a new perspective. A perspective that can shift your life's trajectory from here forward. You are not unlucky, living out some karmic cycle, or not destined for Real Love. All those concepts are untrue and leave you powerless and stuck. It is your birthright to be loved wholly and completely!

When we start healing our shame and unworthiness, Who We Are emerges. We become our True Selves and not some mask-wearing characters our minds concocted in order to be liked. We're willing to shine our divine lights because we want to attract people who align with who we are! These days when I meet a new person, I allow my energy and their energy to do the talking. **I no longer chase, I attract.** My authenticity and self-value do the work for me. People who jive with me and enjoy who I am, pursue me. Those who don't, won't. This saves me valuable time and energy.

The spiritual journey is about returning to the unconditional love already inside us that raises our vibrations and attracts higher quality treatment and situations to us. And... it... works. One hundred percent of the time.

Part Two

Resetting the Foundation –
Let the Healing Begin!

Chapter Three

Retraining Your Brain

Each time you make a new choice that is in alignment with your future, you are priming your brain to install the neurological hardware to actually think, act, and feel the person you want to be in your future.

~ Dr. Joe Dispenza

All you've learned up to this point is a set-up for the upcoming work in this chapter and the ones that follow. Because once you understand the *what and why* behind People Pleasing, the *how to* heal it makes sense. So far, you've learned that your subconscious mind was programmed through direct and indirect messages and influences from your external environment. These are called false or limiting beliefs. These beliefs said you're too much of one thing, not enough of something else, or they warned you of "potential" emotional danger. They disconnected you from the unconditional love within and drained your worthiness cup. You've learned an empty worthiness cup promotes neediness and desperation for love and approval outside of yourself. Your empty cup contributed to the "faulty" foundation you've built your past relationships on, which is why they were dysfunctional, lopsided, and unfulfilling.

To improve our relationships, a foundational reset is required. An engineer who builds skyscrapers knows the foundation they're built upon is crucial. The taller and grander the building, the deeper and sturdier the foundational support must be. The same is true for relationships.

If we desire a deeply connected and healthy relationship, we must build a solid foundation within ourselves first.

Many people believe it's the opposite. They believe if they find the right person "out there," everything "in here" will be okay. The right person will fill the cracks in their heart and make them feel safe, whole, and secure. The issue is that **no one and no thing outside us has this power**. It's an inside job. Period. Additionally, we put a tremendous amount of spoken and unspoken pressure on our loved ones to fill a void they are incapable of filling.

I've seen far too many relationships crumble because one party relied on the other party to make them happy and complete. No matter how honest, loving, and attentive their partner was, it was never enough.

Sometimes this is where infidelity comes from. When Partner A is unable to fill the insatiable void within Partner B, Partner B seeks someone outside the relationship to fill it. Now, I'm not saying you will cheat or your partner will cheat. It's simply a demonstration of what sometimes happens when unworthiness goes unchecked and untended. I've watched many relationships end that might not have, had each partner worked on their respective inner worlds. Many people unknowingly take the easy path of blame rather than turning inward and changing the only person they can—themselves. Resist the urge to feel guilty if any of these situations are familiar to you. You are a work in progress doing the very best you can. It's imperative to remember the past is the past and you are choosing to move forward with empowerment.

Additionally, I've heard many people refer to our healing journeys as "hard" work. The word *hard* signifies using a great deal of force or strength to accomplish a task or goal. I cringe whenever I hear this because (a.) it's not accurate and (b.) it implies a long, difficult, and exhausting journey.

The healing journey is not hard, it's simply different.

We are learning to shift our minds from fear-based thinking to love-based thinking. *Intentional effort* is a better descriptor of the work required. It's acting intentionally about where we put our focus and attention. Rest in knowing your healing path with God will not call you to do anything that feels wrong or outside your integrity. The healing journey is always grounded in the highest vibration of Love. Each step you take in the right direction will feel good. You'll feel lighter, extra expansive, and excited for more!

The only time the healing journey might be described as "hard" is the initial detachment from ego. If a person has functioned long-term in a state of listening to and acting from ego (fear, control, or victimhood), stepping into the unknown can feel awkward and frightening. Remember, the ego doesn't want your healing and will tell you unscrupulous things to keep you from growing. Most of us know Einstein's definition of insanity by now: *Doing the same thing over and over again and expecting different results.* Choosing to heal requires courage to try something different to get new and improved results.

There's a story about a rock climber who was repelling down a massive granite face. The sun was setting and the temperature was rapidly dropping to below freezing. He continued his descent in the cloak of darkness until he reached the end of his rope. He waved his hand below his dangling body and felt only space. He knew if he didn't reach the ground soon, he'd freeze to death. He cried out to God for help. God responded, "Let go of the rope."

The man replied, "What do you mean?! If I let go, I'll die!"

God responded again, "Let go of the rope."

The man refused to let go.

The next morning a couple of hikers happened upon the granite face and saw a man dangling from a rope. He was dead. They reached up and cut the rope to bring him down. He was two feet above the ground.

The ego's job is to keep us safe, and it does so through crafty, ingenious, and clever manipulation to keep us constricted and afraid. It knows following our Divine Guidance will lead to its demise. Therefore, it screams negative and scary things at us because it knows we often listen first to the loudest voice we hear. The letting go that's required is a willingness to open your heart and mind to new perceptions and faith that anything derived from Love/God is always correct. There's no threat of death involved like the ego wants you to think. It's actually the opposite: on the other side of fear is your most prosperous life ever!

Imagine hanging from a tree by an old, dried-out vine that could break at any minute, causing you to plummet to the ground. But within arm's reach is a fresh, new, stronger vine. You're afraid to let go of the vine you're holding onto because it's all you've known. The idea of trying out another vine is scary because it's unfamiliar. To save yourself, you must be willing to put one hand, then the next, then one leg, then the next, onto the new vine. This is what faith looks like—moving one step at a time toward the idea there is something better. No one says you have to swing like Tarzan over to the next vine. A slow transition will do you just fine as the seeds of faith begin to flourish. The more you rely on God/Truth, the stronger your faith will become. This is how we pivot from surviving to thriving!

The healing journey is a hero's journey. It requires a commitment to the desired outcome, faith in the unknown, and dedication and fortitude to see it through.

Fierceness is Required

Continue. Be loving and be strong. Be fierce and be kind.
And don't give in and don't give up.

~ Maya Angelou

Think of someone you love dearly who is weak and cannot defend themselves like a child, elderly person, or a pet. Now imagine someone wanting to harm them. Did you notice that protective feeling rise up in your body? It's the feeling of love combined with an energy of fierceness. I can draw this emotion up quite easily when I picture my children, an elderly loved one, or a defenseless pet. No one gets to mess with them. Not on my watch! Ya feel me?

Now see yourself as a defenseless child who needs your protection. Close your eyes and envision yourself sitting on a park bench next to little You. Sit so close you can feel little You's body heat. Shoulder to shoulder, thigh to thigh. Now take the feeling of fierce protectiveness and turn it toward this little child. Allow it to passionately arise inside you. Sit with it. Embody it. Fill your entire being with it. Wrap your arm around little You's shoulders, pull them close, and tell them that from this point forward you'll do whatever it takes to protect and support them. You will no longer allow them to be mistreated, bullied, abused, unprotected, taken for granted, abandoned, or neglected. Stay with this vision as long as possible. It feels good, doesn't it? It might have even brought some tears. That's because the little You who's felt forgotten, neglected, unprotected, and unloved finally feels like they matter. This is what you've been missing all along.

That vision and feeling kept me moving forward on the healing path. A loving, intense protectiveness of little Kristen illuminated my way. To this day, if someone treats me poorly, I turn to little Kristen and tell her, "I see what's happening here and I haven't forgotten my promise." I immediately experience a sense of calm, much like I would feel having a personal bodyguard. By utilizing this practice, I'm *reprogramming my brain* to know what it feels like to matter and be a priority. I remind myself I am significant, I deserve to be treated well, and I commit to never abandoning myself again.

This may seem like a paltry exercise, and you might be tempted to skip past it. I highly encourage you not to. Each step I'm guiding you through is part of reclaiming your power and filling your worthiness cup. The small child who grew into adult You carried all your fears of inadequacy and false beliefs with you. It's that small and powerless child we are healing. We are resetting the foundation that sweet, innocent child grew from. Some circles call this re-parenting. I've grown quite fond of that term because we are giving to ourselves what was missing in our youth. We are re-raising ourselves to stand on solid foundations. Even if we had loving parents, they weren't perfect. They couldn't be because we're all fallible human beings. And even if they were amazing, they couldn't protect us from how we processed messages from the external world.

I am never about hating on parents who did the absolute best they could with the experiences, knowledge, and beliefs they had. This isn't their jury trial. Like Louise Hay, author of *You Can Heal Your Life* and founder of Hay House Publishing, once said, "If your mother did not know how to love herself or your father did not know how to love himself, then it would be impossible for them to teach you to love yourself. They were doing the best they could with what they had been taught as children."

This is about honoring YOUR experiences and what YOU felt while you were in your formative years. What YOU needed and didn't get. And what YOU need now to heal. We don't have to have abusive and dysfunctional childhoods to grow into People Pleasers. Ironically, not all people raised in dysfunctional environments became People Pleasers. You're reading this book because you've identified a pattern and you're ready to heal it. Pinpointing how it happened or where it stems from might be interesting to explore and uncover, but it's not necessary for healing except sometimes in the case of severe trauma. If you've experienced this type of trauma, your healing may require specialized therapy. I recommend consulting a mental health professional to guide you through.

Reframing Limiting Beliefs

We are addicted to our emotions of the past. We see our beliefs as truths and not as ideas that we can change.

~ Dr. Joe Dispenza

As mentioned before, the ego's job is to preserve itself and to keep itself alive. It will use any means necessary to do this, including fear, bullying, illusions, and lies. The ego/lower self is darkness whereas our God/Higher Self is Light.

There cannot be darkness where there is light.

The ego's greatest foe is God/Truth/Light because that is the only thing that can eradicate it. It will do everything in its power to keep us from awareness and Truth. It's basic psychology that fear is a highly effective way to control people. If you scare someone enough, they'll do exactly what you say. The ego is the gold medal Olympian of fear and knows exactly what to say to keep us afraid, small, and stuck.

In contrast, our Higher Selves only deal with Truth. Truth that reigns from the highest possible love, wisdom, and energetic frequencies. Truth that expands us, grows us, and heals us. Truth that dispels darkness. Truth that always has a peaceful feeling, a resonance, or a "ringing true" associated with it. Truth that is always for the highest good of all concerned. So, with our Higher Selves as available to us as our egos, why is it we listen to the ego more? Because the ego is the first, loudest, and most persistent voice in our heads. You've likely heard the phrase, "the squeaky wheel gets the grease." The same thing applies here. As human beings, our attention often goes where the drama is, unless or until we train it otherwise. And the ego is a drama queen!

Truth is a whisper; fear is a shout.

Since we tend to focus where the commotion is rather than where the peace is, we're more likely to attach to the ego's neurotic rantings above all else. We then become frightened and anxious because we believe they are real. Many of us don't think to question our thoughts; we blindly follow them. I sure did until one magical day I tried something different.

In January of 2011, I was an anxious mess and had been for months. I spent more time with anxiety than I did without it. My chest felt constricted, my heart pounded, my breathing was shallow, and I had difficulty staying focused. On the outside I looked fine, but on the inside I was a wreck. During this time, I was reading and studying spiritual and metaphysical material. Somewhere along the way, I learned that our thoughts create our emotions. Those emotions perpetuate similar thoughts, which then create more of the same emotions. It's a vicious cycle, much like when a computer gets stuck in buffering mode. Around and around and around it goes. I also learned that negativity about the past (regret, remorse, wishing it were different) creates depression and negativity about the future (creating "what if" scenarios) creates anxiety. So, logic said my anxiety was stemming from negative thoughts about the future.

During this time, I was following "The Work" of Byron Katie. Katie's work focuses on questioning the thoughts that make us suffer. Katie is known for her four-question technique combined with a turnaround statement to help us reframe our suffering thoughts into positive, better feeling ones that are *as true as or truer* than the original thoughts. Katie developed a worksheet called "Judge Your Neighbor," where she walks you step-by-step through this process. She also has countless videos where you can watch her do *The Work* with people.

One morning, I felt the familiar body "tells" of anxiety creep in. I paused and asked myself what thought was causing the emotion. It went something like this: *You've been divorced twice and have two baby daddies. No man is ever going to want you.*

So, I questioned it. *Is it absolutely true that no man will ever want me?*

I responded with logic. *That's a bit extreme. There are 7.7 billion people (at that time) on the planet. Out of 7.7 billion people, it's ridiculous to think no one will ever want me.* I could feel the anxiety easing up.

I took it further and found three statements that supported my turnaround.

1. I've never had a problem attracting men.

2. There are many great men who meet and marry women with children.

3. I will be a perfect fit for the right man.

My body relaxed, the tension left my chest and my mind cleared. I felt light, free, and hopeful. It blew my mind that my suffering was created from a thought that wasn't even true! I couldn't wait to do more.

Note: Although I didn't take pen to paper to work through the steps in Katie's process, I was still able to shift my mindset. This may or may not work for you. We are all unique and at different points along our journeys. Be mindful not to judge yourself. Always be gentle with yourself through your process of healing. If you need further assistance with reframing limiting beliefs, I invite you to pop over to Katie's website, *TheWork.com*, and watch her videos or hire a specialized coach or therapist to help you.

From that point forward, I made a dedicated decision to pay attention to when my body alerted me to suffering thoughts. (More on this in an upcoming chapter.) The moment I felt the symptoms of fearful thinking, I asked myself what thought had slipped by my awareness. I identified the negative thoughts and turned each one into a statement that was *positive and as true as or truer* than the original. I was surprised by how simple it was once I got the hang of it. If you open your heart and mind and allow your logical brain to assist you, I believe you'll have the same experience.

I then took it a step further. After I reframed my limiting thought, I'd turn to my left (for no particular reason) as if my ego was standing there. I imagined my ego as a cute little gremlin-type creature that was about two inches tall. I spoke to it. *Thank you for trying to protect me. I know this is your job. But this thought (insert truer thought) is true and yours is a lie. So, I'm choosing to believe the Truth. You can go now.*

And just like that, my ego faded away. That's when I learned how weak the ego truly is. It may be loud and persistent, but it's not strong. We only *believe* it is. What IS strong are Truth and Love. They have the power to heal our hearts, shift our attitudes, and light up the darkest of corners of our minds. And... they have staying power.

Within 48 hours my anxiety was completely gone and around two weeks later the negative, painful thoughts had stopped. I retrained my brain to think in a way that served my future, not defeated it. This is one of the most effective practices I've implemented and utilize to this day. If I'm suffering, I know there's a false or limiting belief causing it and I do the work to heal it.

I later learned per the work of Dr. Joe Dispenza that I had "rewired" my brain. Dr. Joe is a neuroscientist researching the fields of neuroplasticity, quantitative electroencephalogram (QEEG) measurements, epigenetics, mind-body medicine, and brain/heart coherence. He teaches, "when we put our attention behind a thought, we are forming new synaptic connections." He also states, "neurons [nerve cells] that fire together, wire together. And as you begin to learn new information, you biologically wire that information into your cerebral architecture. Learning is the forging of new connections." Repeating new information and new thoughts becomes our new way of thinking. He goes on to say, "remembering is about maintaining and sustaining those connections."

Think back to learning spelling or vocabulary words in grade school. It was through repetition that we "learned" them, and it was through using the words that we remembered them. The same is true when reframing an old thought/belief system into a new one.

As mentioned in Chapter One, Dr. Joe states we have approximately 60,000-70,000 thoughts a day and 90% of those thoughts are the same thoughts as the day before. The same thoughts lead to the same choices, the same choices lead to the same behaviors, the same behaviors lead to the same experiences, and the same experiences lead to the same emotions, which drive the same thoughts. This means we have cyclical and repeated patterns of thinking that contribute to cyclical and repeated patterns of behavior. So, if we want a different experience in life, we must reset the foundation of our thinking. Furthermore, all emotions have energetic frequencies. By shifting into higher thoughts and beliefs, our energetic frequencies rise and our experiences improve. Boom! That's what we're aiming for!

Note: It's impossible to monitor every thought. No one has that kind of time and it's also unnecessary. When starting this process, pay attention to the thoughts taking up the most space and causing the most suffering. These are the ones to clean up first.

The journey to reclaiming our power requires restructuring painful and limiting lies into expansive and abundant truths. You can also fortify your reset by journaling about your positive, truer thoughts, meditating on them, and focusing on them before you sleep. What we think about before sleep is what our subconscious mind marinates on for the next six to eight hours. So, why not make it count? I invite you to get started by following the plan below and don't forget, beloved soul siblings, to have fun with it!

Steps to Reframing Limiting & False Beliefs

1. Get in touch with how your body feels when you're thinking positive and negative thoughts. Familiarize yourself with the different emotions and body signals.

2. Using body signals, recognize when you're feeling depressed or anxious and locate the thought/belief that's contributing to the low feeling. Keep digging until you locate it.

3. Ask yourself, is the thought/belief absolutely true?

4. Find an opposite, truer, and better feeling thought to replace the disempowered one.

5. Repeat the new thought/belief several times until you feel a "click" or a "ringing true." This usually happens around your heart chakra in the center of your chest.

6. Turn to your ego (you can name it if you'd like) and thank it for trying to protect you but tell it you don't need its protection at this time. Tell it that you're going to believe (the new thought or belief) instead. Tell it you're safe and to please leave now.

7. Repeat as often as necessary.

How soon you feel results depends on how in touch you are with your body cues and how dedicated you are to the practice. Don't fret if you don't feel a dramatic improvement right away. We are all different so to compare yourself with my or someone else's results isn't quantifiable. If you're having trouble producing a better feeling thought or belief, invite your Divine Team (spirit guides, guardians, angels, and ancestors) to assist you.

Attitude is the ability to reframe the experience
to empower you to future victories.

~ Irwin Woodward

Chapter Four

The Emotional Guidance System

Emotions are our GPS for life. When we are supposed to do something or not supposed to do something our emotional guidance system lets us know.

~ Author Unknown

As People Pleasers, we put others' needs and wants above our own. We make many choices and decisions with the intent to be liked and avoid hurting others' feelings with little regard to whether we like or are hurting ourselves. We're more concerned with others' well-being than our own. Because of this, we push our emotions aside, ignore our needs and wants, and lose ourselves in relationships.

Connecting to our emotions and receiving what they're telling us is required to advance, expand, and prosper through life. They are the best indicators of what is important to us, what we should pay attention to, how we are treated by others, and how we are treating ourselves. When we don't honor our emotions, we lose touch with a vital guidance system that supports our True Selves and helps us return to a balanced state.

The ability to process our emotions effectively is called Emotional Intelligence (EQ). Many of us were not taught to be aware of, control, or express our emotions in healthy ways. Most likely we were raised by adults who didn't handle their own emotions well, so they couldn't teach us how to handle ours. No shame or blame is intended on them as we can't teach what we don't know. We may have also been scolded or shamed when we cried, sent to our rooms when we were angry or frustrated, or ignored when we were sad. In many cases, you might have been told something like *you're fine, get over it, stop crying, stop being dramatic, you're too sensitive, don't be ridiculous,* or *big boys don't cry.*

Since our emotions weren't validated and were often viewed as inappropriate or bothersome, we perceived them as unimportant or wrong. So, we discounted their value and hid them away in hopes of avoiding judgment or appearing problematic. But in doing so, we lost touch with a fundamental part of our being.

There are two common ways we avoid our emotions. **Repression** is an *unconscious* defense mechanism our brain derives to help us survive environments that are chaotic, unsafe, or painful. The brain *unconsciously* pushes negative emotions, thoughts, and memories out of our awareness. **Suppression** is *conscious* avoidance because we knowingly ignore, stuff, or hide our emotions. Keep in mind that which is unconscious becomes conscious the moment you become aware. And what we are aware of we can work with. (Remember, awareness is key.) Honest self-inquiry and reflection will help you bring what is unconscious forward for healing. If you recognize one or more of the patterns on the list below, you could be consciously or unconsciously avoiding your emotions.

- You feel uncomfortable when people are emotional or express their negative emotions.

- You do not express your negative emotions (in some cases your positive emotions too).

- You believe negative emotions are weak, wrong, or bad and should be kept inside.

- You sometimes or often blow up due to pent-up emotions.

- You distract or avoid negative emotions by using short-term coping or self-soothing behaviors such as, but not limited to, excessive drinking and/or drugs, perfectionism, workaholism, hyper-control, disordered eating, isolation, pornography/sex addictions, or excessive spending.

- You find difficulty admitting when people or situations in your life are hurting you.

- You have difficulty admitting when you are struggling and often describe your current state as "fine."

- You put on a positive front for others.

If you related to one or more of the mechanisms above, give yourself a high five! This is cause to celebrate! You've identified something that is going to shift the trajectory of your life. Wrap your arms around your body and tell yourself you're doing a great job and you're right on track! **Remember, you're securing your inner child.** There is no grading scale or level of good or bad on this journey. Be grateful for whatever mechanism your brain designed to help you survive difficulties in childhood because it served you well. Your brain knew exactly how to get you through. However, the survival mechanisms that served us in childhood often no longer serve us in adulthood.

It's not your fault you weren't taught Emotional Intelligence, but it is your responsibility to learn it now.

As an adult in total charge of your life, it's time to do things in a different way. Remind your inner child that emotions are not dangerous or harmful; they are your friends. They are signals or indicators that guide you. Yes, some are more uncomfortable than others, but what's uncomfortable at first becomes more comfortable as you get used to it.

Why Repression Works Against Us

Unexpressed emotions will never die. They are buried alive and will come forth later in uglier ways.

~ Sigmund Freud

Repressing or ignoring our emotions doesn't mean they disappear. They stay in the body and become the festering underbellies of our existence. They also restrict our ability to connect with others through vulnerable and honest communication. This resistance to openness and vulnerability can cause your relationships to be distant and disconnected. Repressed emotions keep us in the "superficial" aspects of life rather than the deep and meaningful places where true connection and trust forms. In some cases, you may have been seen as insensitive to others' emotions (or their suffering) even if deep inside that's not the case. People may have even left your life because it appears you "don't care." Repressed and ignored emotions may also affect our moods, perceptions of life, personalities, world views, and our bodies through symptoms and illnesses.

Many years ago, I had a partner who I had difficulty connecting with on a deep level. Even though he was a nice person, our relationship felt detached and superficial. I never felt like he cared or that I mattered to him. This partner had gone through a traumatic event in his childhood and developed a coping mechanism that was prohibiting him from processing his emotions and connecting with others. When I asked him what he did with negative emotions, he said, "I swallow them." He demonstrated this to me by swallowing as if he was transferring a piece of food from his mouth to his stomach. This is classified as suppression because he was aware of what he was doing. Because he didn't connect with or process his emotions, he developed unhealthy coping and self-soothing strategies like perfectionism, workaholism, and porn addiction. Those behaviors, combined with a lack of intimacy (true connection), contributed to the breakdown of our relationship.

In another case, a client was confused when his partner told him that it wasn't the *quantity* of time he spent with her, but the *quality* that was missing. He didn't understand her meaning until I broke it down for him. Due to the trauma in his youth, his brain designed an unconscious coping mechanism that minimized and discounted his emotions. In essence, it hurt too much to feel. He not only minimized the importance of his own emotions, but also minimized the importance of his partner's. This result was a failure to connect with himself and with others. When we disconnect from our emotions, we disconnect from others too. This can look like a lack of empathy (even if we care deeply on the inside). Our relationships become topical and lack the true intimacy that promotes security and longevity. The repressed person often feels like nothing is wrong because they're not used to having deep connections in the first place. The partner, however, will feel disconnected and alone.

For those of you who may not feel you repress or suppress your emotions, don't quit this chapter quite yet. There's something here for everyone. You don't have to be repressed or suppressed to dishonor your emotions. Getting in touch with our emotional guidance systems involves not only our ability to feel our emotions, but also our capacity to process them and learn what they are telling us.

What Emotions Are and Are Not

Emotions can get in the way or get you on the way.

~ Mavis Mazhura

Throughout centuries, societies have determined which emotions are acceptable and which ones are not. Oftentimes, these are gender specific. For example, anger and aggression are typically acceptable male emotions, whereas sadness and fear are typically acceptable female emotions. Once again, we were directed by the dictates of society to tell us who we are supposed to be. I'm on a crusade to change this stigma for good. Hear me now, good people, **all emotions are normal and necessary** to every person no matter their gender, race, or religion. My goal in this section is to help you understand the true purpose of emotions and how we can utilize them for personal growth.

When I give talks, I often start out using terms the general public can relate to. In the first section, I used the words *positive* and *negative* to reference different emotions. I'd like to clarify that *negative* does not imply bad or wrong and *positive* does not imply good or correct. There are some emotions that we enjoy and some not so much, but **there are no wrong emotions.** Each emotion is important, purposeful, and created equal. From this point forward I will use terms that I feel better describe certain emotions. I'll be using *light* in place of positive and *heavy or dense* in place of negative.

Listening to Your Body

Listen to your body. Do not be a blind and deaf tenant.

~George A. Sheehan

The human body is an extraordinary structure. Everything contained within it is made for a purpose. Each molecule and cell have specific roles that participate in keeping the body alive. Its optimal state is not merely to survive, it is to thrive. The body thrives in a state of physical and emotional homeostasis or balance. Emotions are part of this genius design. In simple terms, they are chemicals released in the brain in reaction to our thoughts about our internal and external environments. Like the systems of the human body, the emotional guidance system serves a specific purpose. It is designed to give us feedback about what is working and what is not.

Emotions are like gauges on your vehicle's dashboard. One can view them as a feedback system or a report on your environment. Their job is to direct us to what needs our attention. Without emotions, we'd have no method of evaluation. Stepping into a higher energetic version of ourselves requires going within and locating and healing our wounded places. It also requires identifying where we are not honoring and respecting ourselves. This cannot happen if we don't recognize the clues pointing us in the right direction.

These signs show up in what I call "body tells." It's important to become familiar with how certain emotions present in your body. You might notice tension in your neck or chest when you're angry. Your eyelids could feel heavy or droopy when you're sad or hurt. Maybe your voice becomes lower pitched when you're frustrated. Perhaps you can't eat when you're scared or nervous or you develop migraines when you're stuffing heavy emotions. Each of us has certain body tells that help us recognize when we've swung out of homeostasis.

Our body wants us to acknowledge what is happening so we can gain information and course correct. This allows us to discern what choices and decisions would best serve our well-being. In Chapter Three, I shared the process I used to reframe limiting beliefs. My pounding heart and inability to focus were my body tells for anxiety. Without them, I wouldn't have known to question the thoughts I was believing. Recently, a friend told me the back of her head tingles and it feels like there's a dark cloud in her brain when she is frustrated. She learned that is her cue to spend time alone.

A couple of weeks ago I was feeling irritable. I noticed because my shoulders felt tingly and tense, plus my voice was lower and had a minor vibration. I'm not typically irritable, so I recognized these body tells as indicators that something was out of balance. I noted the feeling and made it a priority to investigate it. I discovered that I was irritated by the number of interruptions I was experiencing during my writing time for this very book! Instead of blaming the interrupters (because blame gets us nowhere), I asked myself *what I could do* to rectify the problem. The answer was that I needed to be a better steward of my writing time. This meant scheduling time, turning off my phone notifications, and alerting my family when I'm going to write. And just like that, the irritation left.

You might think I made that look easy. Keep in mind that I've been practicing this for a while and with repetition things get easier. However, that is not to imply that it's always difficult at first. **Your healing journey is uniquely your own.** Allow it to be what it is for you. Refrain from comparing yourself to me or anyone else.

Many people have difficulty identifying body tells and emotions at first because they've been out of touch with them for quite some time. Never fear and do not judge yourself. You are not alone. In fact, you may be surprised how many people are just like you. Your body is yours and with intentional awareness, you'll gain the ability to immediately identify when it's alerting you.

One of my coaching exercises is asking clients to share what emotions they're currently experiencing. Many of them have difficulty naming them. I invite them to describe current sensations in their body and I give them a list of 59 emotions. I ask them to pick out every emotion they're feeling. Each time the client identifies the correct emotion, their physical body starts relaxing. When we're able to sit with an emotion and feel it through, its intensity starts to dissipate. I recently heard it takes approximately 90 seconds for this energy shift to occur. Imagine that! A mere minute and a half can make the difference between storing dense energy or releasing it.

Emotions are Energy

Emotion is energy in motion.

~ Peter McWilliams

When the body has a surplus of something, it works to release it so it may return to a balanced state. The same is true with a buildup of emotional energy. The most common way you've likely already experienced release is through laughing and crying. Those are energetic emissions of happiness and sadness. Both expressions are generally viewed as acceptable. However, expressing heavier emotions tends to be stigmatized, so many people repress or ignore them. The problem is that avoiding heavy emotions creates a buildup of dense energy within our bodies. This buildup can lead to dysfunctional self-soothing or coping behaviors (oftentimes presenting as addictions), an inability to navigate life, or sickness in the physical body.

Heavy emotions can also build up to unmanageable levels until we "lose it" on some unsuspecting person. We might feel better in the moment, as we've released pressure, but it often leaves us to contend with emotions of shame and embarrassment for acting like a jerk. All we accomplished by suppressing (then blowing up) was replacing one heavy emotion with another. Furthermore, shame and embarrassment empty our worthiness cups, and we know by now an empty worthiness cup perpetuates our disempowered behaviors. So obviously, that doesn't work!

During My Tsunami I had so many responsibilities and problems to solve, my well-being was the last of my priorities. I remember going through my days gritting my teeth and feeling ready to explode at any moment. I was so angry at my former husband that my body felt like it was vibrating. I knew I had to release the toxic energy, or I was going to blow. One afternoon while driving alone in my neighborhood, I gave myself permission to feel and express my anger. I wasn't sure what was going to happen, but I was ready to accept whatever came and boy, did I let it rip.

I yelled and cursed out my former husband like no one's business. I growled and screamed and called him every disgusting name I could think of. I felt one tear escape my right eye and run down my cheek.

Then nothing.

Silence.

Stillness.

I remember thinking, *Is that it? There must be more.* I tried to drum up more angry energy, but it was gone. The entire episode lasted about 30-60 seconds. I checked in with my body. *Hmmm... I felt lighter... relieved... and more relaxed.* Although I was still angry with him, I no longer felt the dense energy in my body. My situation was far from over, but I felt better grounded and ready to soldier on. I learned something powerful that day. Releasing emotional energy clears space. There is nothing scary about it and it is safe to do so.

Now, this isn't to say this process will look the same for you. It's simply a demonstration of how feeling our emotions will help them dissipate and free up precious, energetic space. Be aware of the sensations your emotions bring up and remain present with them until you feel them losing strength. Experience them as sensations in your body and allow them to move through.

To this day, if I'm feeling heavy emotional energy well up inside me, I release it by hitting my pillow or mattress or screaming into a pillow. If I feel tears coming, I don't hold them back. If I feel particularly spazzy or hyper, I dance and sing or I play-wrestle with a family member (if they let me, ha-ha). After each release, I am better grounded and ready to carry on with whatever tasks are in my queue.

If you're someone who doesn't (or can't) cry when you're hurt, I'd suggest watching a sad movie or listening to an emotional song and allowing your tears to flow. It's proven that tears released from emotional pain have a different chemical composition than tears released from physical pain. Both serve a particular purpose for the human body. I'm also a big fan of rage rooms. What better way to express built-up frustration, hurt, and anger than to don a safety suit and pummel the crap out of breakable items with a bat? It's a genius invention. You may also try exercising, meditating, drawing, painting, or journaling your emotions. Become your own best advocate and discover what suits you.

Another reason people fear heavy emotions is they're afraid if they allow them, they'll be overwhelmed by them. Others keep them hidden because they're ashamed of feeling the way they do. First, releasing energy has an end. There's only so much to express; it's not a bottomless pit. Imagine holding a blown-up balloon by its nozzle. When you let go of the nozzle, the air escapes. The pressure releases until the balloon deflates. It's still a balloon, but it's relieved of pressure. Emotions fully felt will naturally dissolve. Second, emotions are never wrong and you're not weird for having them. How can we be ashamed of something that is an essential part of being human? That's like feeling ashamed you have eyelids, fingers, or kneecaps. Emotions are fundamental chemical responses to our thoughts. It's vital to give them constructive airtime so we can return to a less pressurized state to make clearer decisions regarding what our next best steps should be.

I devoted an entire chapter of this book to emotions to not only familiarize you with their importance but also to prepare you for the practices in upcoming chapters. Getting in touch with your emotions fills your worthiness cup because you give your inner child what they've always needed—**time, attention, and validation for the way they feel.** Also, by recognizing what you're feeling, you'll know which self-love practice (more on this in an upcoming chapter) to utilize. Much like when the fuel gauge on a vehicle's dashboard shows low, we know to fill 'er up, or when we turn the ignition key and hear a clicking, we know to replace the battery. Emotions will be your guide to what tool or practice is required to reset your foundation. But first, you must learn to connect with them.

Connecting With Your Emotions

1. Check in with yourself once an hour throughout your day. Ask yourself, *What am I feeling physically and emotionally?* Familiarize yourself with sensations in your physical body and connect them with your emotional body. Even when you get good at recognizing your emotions, this is a great daily exercise because it keeps you in touch with yourself.

2. Name the emotion(s). Utilize the list located at the end of this chapter if needed.

3. Sit with the body sensations of the emotion—give them airtime. Release any energy attached in a healthy way that does not impart emotional or physical harm to another person, even if they're the one who upset you. Name the emotion and be intentional with the release. *Important: This isn't about sitting with the thoughts causing the emotion. It's only about releasing the energy of it.*

4. Give yourself a big squeeze and tell yourself what a great job you're doing and how proud of yourself you are.

5. Ask yourself, "What is this emotion telling me?" Examples: Do I need a boundary? Am I grieving? Am I lonely? Do I need rest? Do I need to forgive myself? Should I apologize? Am I thinking mean thoughts about myself? Etcetera.

6. Follow through with action if required or necessary.

If you're a human being, you will experience a myriad of emotions throughout your life. This is a good thing!

Emotions are not your enemies; they are your friends.

Learning to identify them, express them, and receive the guidance they offer is a valuable and lifelong gift. It also tells little You that you're paying attention, you're honoring their feelings and they are important!

Emotions List

Amazed	Foolish	Peaceful
Angry	Frustrated	Proud
Annoyed	Furious	Relieved
Anxious	Grieving	Resentful
Ashamed	Happy	Sad
Betrayed	Hopeful	Satisfied
Bitter	Hurt	Scared
Bored	Inadequate	Self-Conscious
Comfortable	Insecure	Shocked
Confused	Inspired	Silly
Content	Irritated	Stupid
Depressed	Jealous	Suspicious
Determined	Joyful	Tense
Disdainful	Lonely	Terrified
Disgusted	Lost	Trapped
Eager	Loving	Uncomfortable
Embarrassed	Miserable	Worried
Energetic	Motivated	Worthless
Envious	Nervous	Violated
Excited	Overwhelmed	

Chapter Five

Taking Radical Responsibility for Your Life

It's your life—but only if you make it so.

~ Eleanor Roosevelt

Historically, when my romantic relationships ended, I rested knowing I wasn't the bad guy. No one would have accused me of such because the treatment I received was so awful. I was a victim, and that was that. *There's nothing wrong with me. I'm a great person. It's all them! Pfft!* So, it wasn't hard for me to brush myself off and get back in the game. Then one by one I'd attract the same bullshit—different partners with some iteration of disrespect and abuse.

Most of us have heard the phrase, "When you point your finger at someone else, three more are pointing back at you." It's a simple metaphor with a compelling point. I'd be a bazillionaire if I had ten dollars for every time I pointed at the wrongs of others. (Okay, maybe that's a gross exaggeration.) People do crappy things, there's no denying that, and sometimes they're downright insidious. I am not suggesting that people shouldn't receive consequences for their bad choices. Instead, I am suggesting you don't get caught in the blame game trap. This agenda rarely leads us to empowerment. Instead, it keeps us victimized and in low vibe territory.

Weeks after my former husband left the family, I woke up feeling like my old cheerful self. I looked at my calendar and noticed it had only been twenty-one days since he'd left. I was pleased with how great I felt, although it didn't surprise me because I'd mourned the loss of "us" the whole year prior. The part I had to reconcile was losing the dream I had of our future and contending with "starting over." But per my usual resilient self, it didn't take long before I was back on my feet and ready to grab life by the cajones.

During this time, I frequented a restaurant/club down the street from my house where a friend from my high school's rock band played. Every week new high school classmates attended, and it became a reunion of sorts. One night I met a guy I'll call Jacob. We talked, danced, and shared lots of laughs. Around 10 p.m. I was ready to leave. I thanked him for the fun and for restoring my faith in good men. He asked to walk me to my car, and I complied. We exchanged phone numbers and off I went, giving zero hoots as to whether he'd contact me. As soon as I crawled into bed that night, I received a text message from him. He told me he'd be busy traveling for work and play for the next three weeks, but he'd like to get together when he returned. I said it was obvious our schedules weren't going to jive, so let's leave it at that. I thanked him and declined.

He messaged me often throughout those three weeks. It was fun to talk to him, but I wasn't super interested. When he got back, he pushed for a dinner date, and I finally relented. *Oh, why not... he's fun and cute... and we click so well. What's the harm in enjoying an evening?* Long story short—this was the beginning of something very special to me. I never felt so respected and valued as I did by him. He was funny, handsome, sexy, successful, and a loving father to three children. In the following weeks and months, we had dinners, hiked, went to movies, traveled, laughed, sang, and had passionate sex (oh yes, my friends, he even cried once). He told me he loved me about three weeks in and I was equally smitten with him. *This was it! I finally drew a king! It was MY turn to have a great relationship.*

About two months into our relationship, he messaged me and asked if we could meet for lunch. He said he wanted to talk to me about something. I wasn't concerned about what the news might be because we were having such a great time together. After we were settled in our booth and ordered our food, he dropped the bomb.

He was married.

I flew out of the booth and with a laugh in my voice I said, "Are you fucking kidding me? Of course you're married because that's how my life's going right now!" It's hard to describe my emotions at that moment. The night we met he told me he'd been divorced for three years. I was more disappointed than angry, but not overly disappointed because *I* was technically still married as well. I also thought it was sort of charming that he didn't tell me immediately because he didn't want to scare me off. So, how could I judge him?

He looked sad and scared and patted the seat beside him, requesting I rejoin him in the booth. He proceeded to tell me his story. He and his wife married at age twenty because she'd gotten pregnant. He stayed for fifteen years because he thought it was his duty. They'd been separated for three years and had not been together sexually since the separation. Aside from having a divorce decree, he felt divorced.

He went on to say I was the first woman he'd been with sexually since his separation. I believed him because, in the beginning, he was so nervous about sex that it affected him physically (if you know what I mean). I remember asking him if I was the first person he'd had sex with since his "divorce" and he said yes. I also recalled things his friends said to him the night we met. We'd come back from the dance floor holding hands and one of his buddies said, "Look at you, Jacob! Finally!" And then the friend turned to me and said, "We've been waiting a long time for this."

He told me guilt had stopped him from filing for divorce, but now he had a good reason. At this point, I felt like I didn't have anything to lose because they'd been over for years and this appeared to be a logistics thing. We continued dating for approximately six months more, but I could feel something changing. He wasn't as into it as he once was. When I inquired about my feelings, he told me juggling the divorce, kids, work, and me was too much to handle. He needed space to "get his house in order." (Funny how we remember exact quotes when things like this happen.) I asked what that meant for me/us, and he replied, "If you wait for me, my win, but if you don't, which I'll totally understand, my sadness and my loss." He told me this several times in multiple conversations. I'm sure you can guess what I did... I waited.

I gave him the space he requested—no texts, no calls. The waiting was brutal. I loved and enjoyed him so much and missed him terribly. But I had promised to give him space and being the respectful person I am, I did. About two months later, something told me to reach out to him and see how the proceedings were going. With a flippant chill to his voice he replied, "Oh, we've been divorced for over a month." *Ummm, what? Excuse me?* I asked why he hadn't contacted me to let me know. He gave me a lame reason why he didn't want to date me anymore and that was the end. It was over and there was nothing I could do or say to change it. My trusting and loving heart was shattered once again. That's when it really got dark for me.

I always considered myself a strong individual, but two painful betrayals this close together were too much for my heart to bear. I was crushed and completely torn apart. I fell into a state of depression and anxiety unlike anything I'd ever experienced. I sat and stared into space for hours while my kids were at school. I could barely work up the energy to perform my mommy duties. I forced myself to eat only because I felt sick and was losing weight rapidly. I became a shred of the person I used to be.

One day I screamed out to God *Why? Why? Whyyyyy?! Why does this keep happening to me?!* God didn't reply. I vowed with every fiber of my being to remain single and celibate until I figured out how to stop this pattern for good. This was the moment I took radical responsibility for my life and became my own savior. As it turned out, the tiny ember of life force still flickering deep inside me was enough to change my life forever.

In hindsight, I realized something powerful—God/Universe is always listening to what we want. When we ask, it is always given. The problem isn't that we can't have what we want or that there isn't enough to go around. The problem is we aren't energetically aligned to receiving it. God/Universe had heard my desire for a healthy relationship, but also knew I wasn't aligned to receive it. My autopilot/programmed way of thinking, believing, and functioning wasn't an energetic match to a mutually loving and respectful relationship. So, to attract my desire, a foundational reset was required. Continuing to blame my partners, then jumping into new relationships, was only perpetuating my pattern. I *needed* the pain of back-to-back betrayals to humble me and open my heart and mind to something new. In essence, the old me had to "die" to make room for the new me. Like the Phoenix of Greek mythology sets itself on fire to obtain new life, I, too, needed to be reduced to ashes for a rebirth to occur.

Owning Your Part

Accountability is the glue that ties commitment to the result.

~ Bob Proctor

Human beings love to be comfortable. We crave safety and security. We feel best in predictability and familiarity. **We rarely seek change until the pain of staying the same outweighs the discomfort or fear of change.**

I was there. I couldn't take another hit. The pain was excruciating. It was around this time I remembered those critical words my former husband spoke to me: *you are the common denominator*. I realized the error I'd made my entire life was blaming my partners and moving on without taking *any* responsibility. I now know that no matter what the relationship breakdown is, we are part of the equation and contribute to the dynamic on some level.

Their Part + Our Part = Relationship Dynamic

Even if we weren't the "bad guys" per se, we always have a part. The other person may be 80% responsible for the dysfunction but that leaves 20% that's ours. It's that 20% we need to focus on. A common mistake in relationships is trying to get the other person to change or do better. We put all our attention and effort where we have no power because we cannot change other people. The only true power we will ever have is over ourselves. If we don't like the experience we're having, the only true question is, "How am *I* contributing to this situation?"

Have you ever had multiple conversations with a person about their bad behavior and each time they apologized and said they'd do better? They might've been "good" for a couple of days or weeks afterward, then went right back to their old ways. This is because many people will not change unless the stakes are high enough. The problem is that the more time we spend trying to convince them of their errors, the more valuable energy we waste trying to control something we cannot. No manipulation strategy or convincing ever works to change another person until that person is ready to change for themselves.

The only power we have to promote change in our relationships is our own growth and expansion.

True, lasting, and powerful change comes from you! YOU are the only person you can control and that's all the control you need.

Look at a relationship like a math equation. Your side plus their side equals the sum or outcome. I like to demonstrate this with a simple addition problem. Let's say you're a 5 and your person is a 6. (The value of the numbers is irrelevant; they're only for demonstration purposes.)

$$\text{You} + \text{Them} = \text{Outcome}$$

$$5 + 6 = 11$$

Now, 11 (the dynamic between you), is not working. Something needs to change. You believe the other person is the problem (and they very well could be), but you are powerless to change them. The only part of the equation you can change is yours.

I'll use a personal story as an example. I once had a person who raised their voice to me on a regular basis. I repeatedly asked them to stop, but they didn't. I knew I was powerless to change them, so I went within and asked myself: *What can I change about myself? Where can I grow?* I realized when I stayed in the conversation with them, I'd get so frustrated I'd end up yelling back. I was never the one to "draw first blood" so to speak, as I'm not prone to spouting off at people, but I was equally responsible because I was caving in and matching their low vibe energy.

So, the next time this person popped off, I kindly said, "I love you and I want to hear what you're saying. However, I can't listen when your voice is raised. I'm going to hang up now. Feel free to call me back when you can speak gently." I hung up AND I walked away from my phone. (I did that because I knew I'd be tempted to respond to any follow-up texts.) I replaced *my* typical behavior with **a more empowered one**. I upleveled *myself*. The person called back about an hour later and we had a successful conversation. This is what winning looks like, my friends! It's these little victories that contribute to the healing of our relationships. Upleveling *my* behavior changed the equation, which gave us a different outcome!

We are responsible for our well-being. If we don't like the way something is going, it's our job to find a more empowered way to handle it. We must be willing to become our own best friends, advocates, and fierce protectors of our energy. We have the choice to remain at the mercy of others' behaviors or choose higher for ourselves. Resist the ego's urge to convince you this is a "fault" thing. Determining fault doesn't necessarily result in change. Taking responsibility for our happiness and choosing what best supports us does.

Disclaimer: In cases of mental, emotional, and physical abuse, it is best to get you and those dependent on you to a safe environment as soon as possible. There are agencies available that can assist you with your next steps.

Own *Only* What's Yours

The majority of People Pleasers have a history of owning what's not theirs and allowing others to make them question themselves. If you've been in a gaslighting or defensive relationship, you know exactly what I mean. When our self-worth is low, we are malleable to the words spoken to us. But when we're strong and centered in ourselves, their words cannot sway us. This has nothing to do with being stubborn. The path to empowerment is about becoming intimately connected to self. When we know every crack and crevice of our psyche and we heal our disempowered places, we become untouchable by others' sinister attempts to manipulate us. This is one aspect of what healing from the inside out will do for us.

I remember when a former partner accused me of jealousy when he had what I call "gawking syndrome"—staring at attractive women. I am not a jealous person, but I believe gawking at other women is disrespectful to the woman you are with. He attempted to make it my fault by accusing me of insecurity and jealousy. I refused to own his accusations. I wouldn't even consider it. (Before my healing work, accusations like this would've made me doubt myself and back down.) He then accused me of not taking responsibility for my stuff. He was trying hard to be right, bless his little heart, but I was unswayable. I know what insecurity and jealousy feel like in my body, as I'd experienced them in the past, and this wasn't it. His failure to take responsibility didn't mean the responsibility was mine. I made it clear with words and actions I wouldn't be with a man who gawked at other women, and I held my line calmly and assertively. My unwillingness to own what wasn't mine was the catalyst for him to look fully at himself. He eventually understood his behavior was hurting our relationship and he stopped doing it.

As your worthiness cup starts to fill, you'll notice an increased clarity in the way you see relationship situations in your life. No longer will you fall for the manipulation strategies of others designed to make you back down. Your well-being will naturally become your priority and you'll be willing to hold that line. I've been a recovering People Pleaser for over ten years. I've had my share of people telling me who I am and what my motives are. I no longer fall for it. I trust myself, my connection with Source, and my inner knowing above everything. My worthiness cup is full, I know who I am, and I will not own what is not mine. I have a PhD in me, and you can too.

Discovering Our Unconscious Wounds

*The shadow is the greatest teacher for
how to come to the light.*

~ Ram Dass

An unexplored and unhealed mind contaminates the way we show up in relationships. Many of us have functioned through life, albeit innocently, with cracked and dirty windshields that distort the world we see. We see fear instead of love. We see lack instead of abundance. We see doubt and uncertainty instead of trust. We blame others, withhold honesty and authenticity, fear rejection, and attempt to control. We call this distorted view "reality," and we react to what we believe to be true. Never once have we thought to question it.

During my *College of Kristen*, I was hell on fire to fix whatever had kept me in the cycle of lopsided and painful relationships. Somewhere along the way, I'd learned the concept of psychological projection. Projection is aptly named, as its purpose is to cast an image outward onto something else much like a movie projector. With psychological projection, instead of the image showing up on a movie screen, it shows up in our judgments of people around us. These images are projections of our rejected emotions, traits, and behaviors. They are parts of ourselves we've locked away for fear of society's disapproval. Swiss psychiatrist Carl Jung referred to this collection of our repressed identities as "the shadow."

A simple example is a cheating person who doesn't trust their partner and/or repeatedly accuses them of cheating. The projection is: *I accuse you of being untrustworthy because I am untrustworthy.* Another example is judging someone for impatience. *I accuse you of impatience because I am impatient.* Or something like this: *I accuse you of wanting attention because I want attention, or I accuse you of spending too much money because I spend too much money.* Most often when we're judging another person, we're projecting a disowned aspect of ourselves. I can always discern the difference between a judgment and an observation by the way it feels in my body. Judgments feel prickly and constricting whereas observations feel neutral and light.

Another way to identify projections is by paying attention to what you believe others are thinking about you. He thinks I'm stupid. She thinks I'm boring. He thinks I'm not fun. She thinks I'm a loser. He thinks I'm not attractive enough. Then turn those thoughts around to self. *Do I secretly think this about myself? Do I think I'm stupid? Do I think*

I'm boring? Do I think I'm not fun? Do I think I'm a loser? Do I think I'm not attractive enough?

Much like physical pain directs us to where our body is wounded, our projections direct us to where we're emotionally wounded.

Projections provide an easy and effective way to locate our hidden shame and unworthiness. It might sound weird, but I geek out on this stuff because the freedom and peace I received through this process changed my life!

You might be thinking, eh, I've functioned long enough without dealing with this shadow thing. Is this going to help me have a loving relationship? Can't I just practice self-love and boundaries? Self-love and boundaries are paramount to recovering People Pleasers and I go into them at length in the following chapters. However, there's no quick fix or magic pill for people pleasing recovery. Although doing some of the work will yield amazing results, why stop there? Why not go for the whole shebang?!

When we bring our unconscious wounds forward for healing, our energy naturally improves, and we see life more clearly. It's like massive windshield wipers came into our minds and cleared the gunk distorting our views. Where we were once blind, we can now see. No longer will we see ourselves or others through the filters of our unhealed selves. No longer will we be driven by unconscious fears. No longer will we cling to others for approval because we've healed the wounds causing the behaviors.

Exercise:

Healing The Shadow

1. Pay attention to all judgments about other people (positive and negative). Catch each one as it arises.

2. Ask yourself, "Do I see this trait/behavior/emotion within myself?" Complete self-honesty is required.

3. If the answer is yes, give yourself a warm pat on the back and congratulate yourself for your bravery. (Do not skip the pat! You're retraining your brain that self-honesty and awareness is a good thing.) Then move to Step 4. If the answer is no, ask yourself again. If it's still no, you can release it and move one.

4. Open your heart and send healing love (acceptance, forgiveness, and compassion) to that disowned part of you. Fill your heart with Love, then repeat this mantra: *[Your Higher Power], I see my wound/fear clearly now. I am willing to heal this disowned part of myself. I am willing to become the best version of me I can be. I claim full and complete healing. Thank you for unconditionally loving me. And so it is. Amen.*

You'll not only be surprised how quickly your projections heal, but also how much more compassionate and understanding you'll become to others. Self-healing has a remarkable ripple effect. Since we are all connected, what we heal within ourselves will help to heal the world. By staying committed to this practice, I noticed a peace enveloping my life that surprised and astounded me. A peace that I'd never experienced before. This peace rippled out and not only did life become easier to navigate, my relationships became more serene.

Fun Fact: Not only do we project our darkness, but we also project our light. Have you ever noticed how loving, kind, generous, or sweet someone is? Did it elicit warm feelings inside you and perhaps make your eyes well up with tears? Those are emotional responses to positive projections of yourself. **It is as important to own your positive traits** as it is to own your negative ones. Taking responsibility means taking accountability for **all of your pieces and parts**—not just the dark, but the light too!

> *The shadow work is the path of the heart warrior.*
>
> ~ Carl Jung

Emotional Triggers

> *Healing happens when you're triggered and you're*
> *able to move through the pain, the pattern, and the*
> *story and walk your way to a different ending.*
>
> ~ Vienna Pharaon

Much like projection, emotional triggers are the body's way of alerting us to wounded parts of ourselves that need our attention. My first experience with emotional triggers was when I was a little girl. We had a neighbor named Steve. My mom told me and my brothers to never approach Steve quietly from behind. She said he'd likely turn around and punch us or hurt us in some way. (This scared the bejeezus out of us.) She went on to say that Steve was in "the war" (she didn't specify which one) and he was stuck in high-alert mode because he had to constantly watch his back so an enemy wouldn't sneak up on him. Today this is known as Post Traumatic Stress Disorder or PTSD.

An Emotional Trigger or PTSD is the result of an extraordinarily stressful event that shatters your sense of safety and security. My simple definition is *any stressful event that emotionally rocked your world.* I want to emphasize that emotional triggers don't only come from major catastrophic events like battlefields, car crashes, house fires, or the unexpected deaths of loved ones. They can come from any event that your brain processed as emotionally or physically threatening. Additionally, what emotionally rocked your world may not rock another person's world. How we process tough emotional situations is unique to each individual. What was painful and traumatic for one person may not have been for another. Their brain may have handled the same situation differently due to their unique DNA, personality, and experiences. This is why siblings raised in the same environment often have different realities.

Sadly, bad things happen to good people every day. There's likely no one on Earth who hasn't been victimized via the words or actions of another person. I feel it's accurate to say we've all been victims and experienced trauma in some form. I'll never discount or excuse the dastardly acts bestowed upon anyone. They were despicable and wrong and in no universe would they ever be okay. Each of us is so unique that it is unjust to say one person's trauma trumps someone else's. If an individual's brain processes an event as traumatic, then it's traumatic. Period. We have the wounds and triggers to prove it, **and** it's our responsibility to heal them.

You might be thinking, "No, no, no, you don't understand. My trauma was really bad, it's not possible to heal it. It's worse than anything anyone's experienced." I understand the temptation to make your situation "special," as that's what the ego wants you to think. It *wants* you to believe no one understands. It *wants* you to think you have a right to stay in victimhood. It *wants* you to believe you can't get better. That way you won't process and heal. Remember, the ego's job is to keep itself alive, and awareness and Truth are its Kryptonite.

Somewhere mid-Tsunami, I found myself hovering over an abyss of victimhood so alluring that if I chose to jump in, I'm not sure I'd have gotten out. After all, I had a reason to feel this bitter and resentful. It was true! I'd been disrespected, dishonored, and abused repeatedly by friends and partners. Enough was enough! No one would blame me. How could they? The facts were all there! (Said my ego...)

But my soul was saying something else. It said that if I chose victimhood, then my abusers would win. *Oh, man, I didn't like that one bit.* A fierceness like I had never experienced arose inside me. There was no way I was going to let those assholes win. What they did was unacceptable and wrong, and it would never be okay. I remember this day clearly. It was an average day just like any other **and** it was the day I chose victory over victimhood.

How Triggers are Created

When a traumatic event happens, the memory of it embeds in our subconscious minds. This happens in the part of the brain called the amygdala. The amygdala (or reptilian brain) is responsible for keeping a lookout for fearful or threatening stimuli. Its job is to store information regarding traumatic events and scan our environments for indicators of potential threats. To paraphrase Dr. Joe Dispenza, the brain doesn't know the difference between what is happening in reality and what is happening in thought. So, when it spots something that mimics a past trauma, a surge of fear, panic, and an automatic reaction of "fight, flight, or freeze" occurs. This is what we call being "triggered." The triggered individual has an automatic, knee-jerk reaction to either attack (fight), walk or run away (flight), or to detach or hide (freeze).

For example, I once had a client who verbally attacked his wife when she asked commonplace questions like, *What time will you be home from work? Will you come snuggle with me? Can you please turn off that light?* This gentleman had been traumatized by a previous partner who left him unexpectedly. On her way out the door, she told him all the ways he'd "failed" her. She had never communicated her needs during the relationship, so he assumed all was well. Therefore, her abrupt departure came as a massive shock. This event left a painful mark on his psyche. It remained hidden away until his new partner made requests of him that triggered his internal security system. *Red Alert! Red Alert! You're not doing enough! She's going to leave you!*

His brain processed her requests to mean he was failing in the relationship. Since his triggered response was to fight, he'd verbally attack her. He was also slow to take responsibility for his actions because internally he felt "owning it" meant the failure was true. Ironically, his fear of losing her almost became a self-fulfilling prophecy because she couldn't handle his emotional eruptions any longer. Gratefully, he was open to healing his wounded places and they're going strong to this day.

Healing Trauma Triggers

You've likely heard the phrase, "She/he really knows how to push my buttons!" Many of us mistakenly believe the problem is that other people push our buttons. Because in our minds, if they didn't do the thing that caused our harsh reaction, there wouldn't be a problem. Right? Nope. Not even close. **It's not people touching our buttons that's the problem, it's that we have them in the first place.** It is our responsibility to heal our wounds, not for others to tiptoe around them.

No one can heal our wounded spaces but ourselves. Nor should we require others to walk on eggshells around us because (a.) eggshell walking enables us to continue the behavior and (b.) it puts a tremendous amount of pressure on our loved ones. Imagine having to maneuver around a bunch of eggshells scattered on the floor. If you're off guard for one minute you'll likely crush one, then BAM the fight is on! That's an exhausting way to function within a relationship. If you've been on the receiving end of eggshell maneuvering, I'm certain you can relate. I can only speak for myself when I say, I don't want people to have to work that hard to be around me. I want people to have a pleasing experience when they're with me. This can't happen if they're navigating a minefield of my unhealed wounds.

My husband and I had been together about four years when one evening his behavior touched a wound I thought was healed. He and a few friends had gone up to a buddy's cabin to enjoy a night of food, card games, and male bonding. I was so happy he was going! Not only because I knew he'd enjoy it, but also because my little one and I got to have girl's time. Around 10 p.m. the electricity went out at our house. I called my husband to let him know and ask about possibly resetting the breaker if needed. He didn't answer my call, nor did he respond to my follow-up texts. Boom! Triggered. Intense emotions arose inside of me. I wanted to attack him for not responding. I wanted to make him wrong!

But I knew a thing or two about wounds and triggers by this point, so I asked myself what was going on. It was obvious. My former husband was up to infidelity shenanigans when he was away from home. I knew something was amiss because he wouldn't respond to my texts or calls. And when he did finally reply, he was cold and short and acted like I was bothering him. So, when my current husband didn't answer my call, my brain said, *Alert! Alert! He's up to no good!*

My husband called me about an hour later, innocently and kindly telling me he left his phone inside when he went outside to start a fire in the fire pit. While he was out there, the guys came to join him. They got to talking and he lost track of time. I heard him, I believed him, but my body was still reacting. I took a deep breath and did my best to keep my tone and volume calm. I said, "Okay... I need you to know I am totally triggered right now and I'm going to tell you how to handle this. Tell me you're not up to no good and everything is okay."

He did what I asked, but the typically talkative me didn't say a word. I sat in silence knowing if I opened my mouth it wasn't going to be pretty.

This was the only time he'd seen me triggered and he was confused by what was happening. I'd explained to him how triggers work, but he didn't understand. (He was very new to this type of information.) He asked if he should come home and although my fear was screaming YES!, I knew that would only enable my wound. I replied, "No, please stay. I just need a couple of minutes to remind myself that this is an old story, and you are not him." We hung up the phone and I sat on the edge of my bed and talked myself through my trigger until the dense energy released from my body.

I'm happy to report that I no longer have that wound; I did the work required to heal it. Many people believe that healing past trauma is difficult, and in some cases, that might be true. But it's important to know as human beings we are all capable of healing. We might need assistance from a mental health professional to heal certain traumas, but there's much we can do to heal ourselves. There's no shame in whether or not you can overcome this by yourself. Be honest with yourself on your healing journey. If you find you need help, be your own advocate and seek appropriate support.

Exercise:

Healing Your Triggers

1.   Become aware of your triggers. What events/ situations make you automatically react in either fight, flight, or freeze?

2.   Recognize when you are triggered. You'll know you're triggered by your intense emotional response that is often accompanied by an inner panic feeling. Say to yourself, "I am triggered." Repeat this to yourself over and over until you feel a decrease in intensity.

3.   Pause. Sit with the feeling. Resist the urge to push it away or blow up on someone else.

4.   Ask yourself if you absolutely know this is happening or if this is a reminder of a past experience.

5.   Consult the character of the person who touched your wound. Are they doing what you think they are doing? Ask yourself: *Is it true _____ is doing _____? Is this like them? Am I seeing this clearly or through my wounded self?*

6.   Repeat this to yourself: *That was my old reality. The past is over, and I am safe now. This person is not that person. All is well.*

Through the six steps above, we're creating space between the triggers and our knee-jerk reactions. We're bringing what's embedded in our unconscious minds forward to our conscious minds where we can apply logic and reason. We cannot work with what is hidden in our unconscious minds, but we can work with what becomes conscious.

Your trauma triggers may not be healed in one sitting. You may need to repeat this process several times to reduce your triggered response to a manageable level. It may also help to enlist your loved ones to assist you with this process if you feel safe doing so. Do not look for perfection or judge yourself if a particular trigger keeps arising for you. Healing our wounds often resembles peeling away the layers of an onion. One by one you'll remove another layer to reveal the healing beneath. As I worked through my practice, the intensity of each episode consistently decreased. Occasionally I'll still feel triggers arise, but they are minimal and much easier to handle.

I don't claim to be a psychiatrist, nor am I a mental health professional. I'm a woman who set a course to heal my heart and mind and achieved remarkable results. You, my beloved soul sibling, are in charge of your healing journey. Only you truly know what you need. If you feel you need a little more than this chapter offers regarding healing trauma-induced wounding, I encourage you to seek additional guidance and assistance.

The way I see it, we're all a bunch of tiny baby humans toddling around in our Earth suits doing our best to figure this place out. Sometimes we hit the mark and sometimes not so much. What I know for sure is we cannot change anyone other than ourselves. When we take full and complete responsibility for ourselves, we clean up our side of the equation. We raise our energetic vibrations, become who we are meant to be, and stop taking the crap dished out by those stuck in fear and control.

This doesn't mean we become "better" than anyone else. We are all divine sparks of God on our unique spiritual journeys. The best thing we can do for the greater good of all concerned is to work on our side of the equation by continuing to evolve and grow. Taking full responsibility for all aspects of our lives will ultimately lead to reclaiming our personal power and upleveling our experiences.

Chapter Six

The Miracle Cure

You really have to love yourself to get anything done in this world.
Love yourself first and everything else falls into line.

~ Lucille Ball

When I considered my intention for this book, I envisioned a pathway taking people from where they are to where they want to be. I saw in my mind's eye an arched cobblestone bridge traversing the gap from shame and unworthiness to empowerment and freedom. The engineering of a cobblestone bridge is vitally important to its durability and longevity. Each bridge has a keystone (a specifically shaped stone) located at the apex of the masonry arch. It is the final piece placed during construction that locks all the stones into position. This allows the bridge to bear weight. Although the keystone bears the most weight, the cobblestones working with the keystone are equally important to complete the structure. **This chapter is the keystone to your people pleasing recovery** and the chapters preceding and following it are significant parts of the entire unit.

This book is a replication of the work I did during my *College of Kristen* and continue to practice to this day. It is the bridge from where you are to where you want to be. If I was granted one wish for what I'd like you to take away from this book, it would be this chapter. What you're about to learn is the remedy to your empty worthiness cup. It is the miracle cure for shame and unworthiness. I am bold enough to guarantee if you diligently apply the practices in this chapter, your energetic vibration and life will dramatically improve for the better. Like any area of our lives we want to improve, dedication and effort are required. The only question is, how willing are you to put forth the effort to achieve results?

Healing our self-worth is not something anyone can do for us.

There are no shortcuts, magic pills, or quick fixes. True healing is about taking responsibility for all areas of our lives. It's about releasing victimhood and becoming our own heroes. It's about giving ourselves what we tried in vain to get from others. It bums me out when I see influencers sharing dating and relationship hacks (aka manipulation strategies) to get the guy or girl. Although they may get short-term results, they're not enough to sustain a long-term, healthy relationship. I find them a huge waste of time for anyone who wants a mutually loving and supportive relationship. The work required is never about moving chess pieces on a board. It's about true healing from the inside out. When we fill our worthiness cups, *we'll naturally show up* in ways that demonstrate our true value and essence. No strategies or hacks will be required because your worthiness will organically work through you.

Becoming an empowered individual requires training. I liken it to conditioning for a 10K race. It's unlikely we'll wake up one day and magically have the toned muscles required to finish the race without putting in the work. It takes one purposeful action step at a time toward your goal. The same is true for self-worth recovery. With each intentional step, it becomes easier as you build momentum and endurance. And much like physical training, you'll immediately notice improvements.

Healing your self-worth is not a one-and-done kind of thing; it is a way of life. It is the foundation that will connect, lock, and support the entire structure of your personal empowerment. No longer will you have to *force* yourself to be strong and empowered. Force requires significant energy expenditure, which is unsustainable long-term. That's why we can only "be strong" for so long. True self-worth is not something we can fake our way through because eventually we'll get tired of holding up the façade and our unworthy self will come rushing back. True shame and unworthiness healing dissolves our disempowered patterns and changes the way we show up to life.

The Most Important Relationship

*Your relationship with yourself sets the tone for every
other relationship you have.*

~ Robert Holden

The most important human relationship we'll ever have is the relationship with self. Our entire life and all other relationships grow from this foundation. Garden soil that's nurtured bears the sweetest fruit and the same is true for you. When we love ourselves unconditionally, we show up more empowered and we relationship in an improved way. We no longer need others to provide our worth because we already know we are worthy. This also reduces hidden expectations and takes the pressure off our loved ones to fill the voids they were never capable of filling in the first place.

No one outside of us has the ability or competence to complete us.

Only we can complete ourselves. We raise our vibrations when we stop looking to others to deem us worthy and we give worth to ourselves instead. Partners and friends become cherries on top of our already happy and fulfilled lives when we stop making them responsible for our happiness. We become clear about the treatment we require, and we're willing to set and maintain healthy boundaries. We love ourselves so much we'd rather be alone than be in poor company.

Prior to my healing work, I remember how often I'd question myself when I was treated poorly. Because I didn't respect, honor, and love myself, there was no clear defining line for when others weren't. Their poor treatment somehow felt "normal." I know now it's because their treatment of me resembled *my* treatment of me. Intellectually I knew their treatment wasn't okay, but something inside me felt wobbly, weak, and unable to set unwavering boundaries. The good news is, when we treat ourselves well, poor treatment stands out like a tornado siren blaring through a small town. There's no more confusion about it! You know who you are and what your value is, and you won't accept anything less.

Our Intrinsic vs. Extrinsic Value

Recognize your own worth and you won't be
drawn to those who don't see it.

~ Doe Zantamata

I invite you to take a minute and write a list of what you think makes you valuable or attractive. I'll wait right here while you do...

Now peruse your list. If you included things like: I make good money, I own a home, I'm educated, I'm financially successful, I'm sexy, handsome, pretty, or drive a nice vehicle, crumble that list up and toss it in the bin! Yep, you heard me. Those things do not define your true value. They are extrinsic possessions you have acquired in your life or physical characteristics you have, but they are **not your true worth**. They're also not guaranteed to always be there, so what happens if you lose them at some point? Will you no longer be valuable?

Society has conditioned us to believe if we acquire certain things or reach certain physical or material goals, we are worthy. It's one of the reasons why we've struggled for so long—we're looking for worth in all the wrong places. It's also why advertising is a multibillion-dollar industry. Advertisers appeal to our unconscious beliefs that we must have "things" (fancy items, youth, wealth, beauty, status) to stand out, be recognized, and be worthy of love, approval, and attention. We buy into this notion and spend piles of money hoping to feel better. It might work for a short while. But when the shine wears off, we are left with the same unworthy feelings we had before, and we soon start searching for our next "hit."

Of course, human beings are primal by nature, and when looking for a mate we are physically attracted to some people more so than others. We can't help who or what we are attracted to. External beauty is in the eye of the beholder and there is someone for everyone. However, physical traits and material gains are not how you are guaranteed to attract *quality* people to you; your empowered vibration is. If we want deeper, more meaningful relationships, we must **intentionally focus** on what our True Worth is.

Remember in Chapter One when God asked me if I'd be my best friend? It's time to answer this question for yourself.

Would you be your best friend? If yes, why?

Take a moment to ponder this question and make a list of all the reasons why. Leave out anything related to the material world. I've placed an Intrinsic Values List at the end of this chapter to assist you. Place a checkmark next to each trait you possess. I invite you not to skip this exercise, as it can be quite powerful. I'll wait here while you do it.

I'm fairly certain you checked at least half or more of the list, didn't you? How'd I know? Because People Pleasers are often warm-hearted earth angels who've fine-tuned what it means to be a good person. Remember, I see you, soul sibling. Now, look at the item titled "Child of God." Did you notice this item was already checked for you? That's because it is **your ultimate, non-negotiable true value** and the only thing that truly matters. You are already and always have been worthy because you are an individual aspect of God. You are Spirit in an Earth suit or "Deity Individuated" as Neale Donald Walsch, author of *Conversations With God*, has been known to call us. This is a fixed fact. You came here with the highest form of worth there is! You simply forgot who you are.

Love is the Answer

Shame and unworthiness are an epidemic on this planet. We are the walking wounded. Everyone has experienced trauma, heartbreak, betrayal, and suffering on some level. We have the emotional wounds to prove it. We'd love more than anything to cure this affliction, but we weren't taught how. Luckily, there is a simple spiritual cure.

**Shame and unworthiness are the dis-ease and
self-love is the miracle cure.**

Pop culture is really pushing self-love these days. This is good because people are becoming more aware, and it's not-so-good because the true power of self-love has been misrepresented and diluted. Many people are forcing themselves to be strong, attempting to control situations and snapping their fingers in a Z formation in the name of self-love. I do applaud their attempts; however, those actions are constructs of the ego, and where ego is, Love is not. Self-love produces a different effect than what the ego does. Self-love results in behavior that is soft but firm. Honorable yet boundaried. Kind yet assertive. Strong yet vulnerable. Humble yet confident. Behavior rooted in self-love doesn't have to *try* to do anything; it just is.

Love is *the most powerful force* in the Universe. Love is God and God is Love. There is nothing greater; there never has been and there never will be. Love is the highest possible energetic frequency, and it has the power to heal all that it's applied to. Where God is, there cannot be ego, fear, control, or manipulation. Anything rooted in Love is always the highest action we can take. Ego emptied our worthiness cups and self-love fills them!

The ego/lower self is rooted in fear. When we listen to its hysterical rantings, we lose our way. God/Higher Self is rooted in Love. When we apply Love to our wounded spaces again and again, we reset our foundations. Here's what's more amazing: there is no opposite of God/Love. Some people claim that hate and fear are the opposite of Love but hate and fear are finite, whereas Love is infinite. What is infinite can have no opposite. What I'm saying is, an ant doesn't stand a chance against an elephant. When Love is in the room, the ego has no choice but to back down.

When I started my healing journey, I vowed to little Kristen to do everything possible to honor, protect, and nurture her. I began treating her with the respect and love she deserved. I gave her the same loving treatment I so freely gave everyone else. It wasn't long before I noticed how different I felt. It was like dropping an eighty-pound backpack I had no idea I'd been carrying. I felt light, peaceful, and free. I never realized how much time and energy I spent trying to be all things to all people and worrying if others liked me. I noticed how different I felt so I asked myself what had changed. At that moment, I realized I knew my true worth for the very first time. I now know how valuable I am no matter what anyone says.

You may be wondering if self-love works for everyone. YES, my friend, YES! We may be unique in our physical design, but the core of who we are is the same—God's children. There's no order of hierarchy or specialness amongst God's children, no matter what race, religion, or gender we are. The self-love remedy is not specified for only a select group of humans. **We are all Love, and we are all Loved beyond measure.** Our inner healing happens when we return to the unconditional Love of God within us. We do this by applying the principles of God/Love to ourselves. This is where it gets super exciting!

The 5 Tenets of Self-Love

First, let's break down the meaning of self-love. *Self,* meaning "of you." *Love,* meaning "of God." Self-love means giving yourself all things that God is. The Love of God is constant. There's no beginning, end, or separation. However, we are Spirit in physical bodies, with thinking minds, having human experiences. We have free will whether we choose to commune with God or with ego. Since the ego is a loud bugger that demands much of our attention, we tend to listen to it more often. By understanding the voice of ego tells lies and the voice of God tells Truth, it's logical to see we've been listening to the wrong voice. Shifting our attention from fear-based thoughts to love-based thoughts is where our healing occurs. Self-love calls for applying all things of God to self—Forgiveness, Compassion, Acceptance, Supportive Self-Talk, Protection, Priority, and Care. It means choosing thoughts and actions that build us up rather than break us down.

People Pleasers focus on their perceived shortcomings and feel ashamed because of them. We try to rid ourselves of shame by overcompensating in our relationships or using unhealthy coping strategies. This causes our energy to fragment and shoot off into many directions rather than where it serves us best, within. Dr. Joe Dispenza says, "Where attention goes, energy flows." The path to empowerment requires pulling the energy we've focused outward back to ourselves with **intentional focus**. The second we choose something different for ourselves, we pivot and change course. Instead of trying to be everyone else's saviors, we become our saviors first.

A change in perception creates a change in direction.

Earlier in this book, you learned how emotions are indicators of what needs your attention. Becoming consciously connected to your emotions (especially the heavy ones) will alert you to when self-love is required. The more committed you are to recognizing what you need, the quicker you'll be at applying the remedy. With consistent effort, your default thinking will shift from small and disempowered to expansive and worthy!

Tenet One—Grace and Forgiveness of Self

*It is very important for every human being to forgive herself
or himself because if you live, you will make mistakes—
it is inevitable. If we hold on to the mistake, we can't see our
own glory in the mirror. We can't see what we're capable
of being. You can ask for forgiveness of others, but
in the end the real forgiveness is in one's own self.*

~ Maya Angelou

Making mistakes is part of being human. We are imperfect and fallible beings. For as long as we roam this Earth, we will make mistakes. It's guaranteed and it's inevitable. To condemn yourself for your mistakes is to hold yourself to an unrealistic standard; a model of perfection that can never be achieved. At the root of perfectionism dwells shame and unworthiness. We unconsciously believe if we're perfect, we'll be loved and valued. When we hit the mark, we're ecstatic, but when we miss, we're devastated and ashamed. Relying on the outer world to validate our worth perpetuates our disempowered cycles. We don't yet understand that the problem isn't our imperfections, it's that we're depending on others' approval to grant us worthiness.

Our souls chose to come here to learn. Our experiences and relationships are our curricula. Mistakes are common while learning. Condemning ourselves for our mistakes is like judging a baby learning to walk. Their first unassisted step (and many, many thereafter) result in falling down. They fall because they haven't yet mastered what they're learning. The same is true for us. Sometimes adults fall because we're still learning. Interestingly, we don't judge babies for their errors because we know they're doing the best they can. In fact, we celebrate each little attempt! Yet as adults, we tend to beat ourselves up for any missteps we make. All of this to say, the problem is not that we make mistakes, it's how we handle them that matters. Our free will affords us the choice to beat ourselves up (ego) or give ourselves grace and forgiveness (God).

Some might argue, "Yeah, but I could've done better!" Yes, we all have the *potential* to do better, but at that moment that's as good as it got. If we could've done better, we would have. People have difficulty owning their mistakes because they fear it will validate the hidden belief that "something is wrong with me." Nothing is wrong with you because you make mistakes. If anything, it makes something right with you because it shows you are a beautiful human being and not a robotic machine.

Loving yourself requires relinquishing the heavy weight of self-condemnation and forgiving yourself for all errors, past, present, and future. When you forgive yourself, you are loving yourself the way God loves you. Forgiveness is of God; Forgiveness is of Love. Our Loving Source does not "grant" us forgiveness—it's already built into the essence of Love. We are forgiven before the mistake even occurs. You are forgivable because you are God's child—you are Love and you are Loved. This is indisputable. It's not God's forgiveness that will let you off the hook; it is your own. Self-love practice involves learning to forgive yourself for your missteps the moment you make them.

Exercise:

Clearing the Energy of Past Mistakes

1. Position yourself in a quiet, solitary place where you won't be disturbed. Close your eyes and imagine the golden white light of God's love filling the room.

2. Get in touch with the shameful actions and behaviors of your past. Invite them to enter the room. Watch as each one moves from the darkness into the light.

3. Focus on one event at a time. Summon it to stand before you. Ask yourself if you did the best you could at that time with where you were in life. (The answer is always yes.)

4. Say to yourself: *I did the very best I could at that time. I release this mistake to [Your Higher Power] to be transmuted from darkness to light. I am open and willing to do better next time. And so it is. Amen.* Repeat as often as needed until you feel it release. Imagine the shame of the mistake floating to the heavens until you can no longer see it, much like releasing a helium balloon outside.

5. If any mistake or shameful place is particularly resistant, use this prayer to invite God/Universe to help you: *[Your Higher Power], I am willing to be willing to forgive myself for my error. I'm willing to love myself as you do. I'm willing to set myself free through forgiveness. Help me to do better next time. And so it is. Amen.*

6. Apologize and request forgiveness from anyone you've hurt or offended. You may do this telepathically if they're no longer in your life or your presence could harm the individual. Bring them to mind, take responsibility for your actions (without excuses), request forgiveness, and let it go. Whether or not they choose to forgive you *does not* determine your worth. It's your forgiveness of self that will shift your energy.

A Course in Miracles refers to this process as The Atonement. It involves correcting the perceptions of our errors, being willing to do better, and raising our vibrational frequencies in the process. Any error atoned for wipes away the fear/dense energy that's standing between you and your Higher Self. It frees you from the imprisonment of guilt to move you forward with empowerment.

Daily Self-Forgiveness Practice

1. Take rapid personal responsibility the moment you realize your mistake. Personal responsibility is a high vibrating, rockstar move and can stop a misstep from exploding into something bigger.

2. If applicable, apologize, ask forgiveness, and make amends with any person(s) you've hurt or offended.

3. Ask yourself what this situation taught you. Often when we learn the lesson the mistake taught us, we won't repeat the mistake.

4. Give yourself forgiveness and grace (let yourself off the hook) for the mistake. Repeat this statement as often as needed until you feel your resistance decrease: *[Your Name], you did the very best you could at the time. You are human and you will make mistakes. You are Love and you are Loved. Everything is okay. You are forgiven.* (Say it like you mean it! Little You needs to know they're not fatally flawed.)

5. Take it to God/Universe: *[Your Higher Power], please return me to my Right Mind so I can move forward with clarity and peace. Please help me choose correctly next time. And so it is. Amen.*

6. Release and move on.

Alexander Pope once said, "To err is human; to forgive is Divine." We are spirits having a human experience. We were put here to expand our souls. By forgiving ourselves quickly and giving ourselves grace for our process, we free up valuable energy to focus on where it'll better serve us. Through grace and forgiveness, we're extending acceptance to our inner child who's felt flawed and broken. There's nothing to condemn ourselves for when we are doing the absolute best we can. Moreover, little You needs to know they are worthy despite being fallible and imperfect. You are going to make mistakes and that is okay. What you do *after* the mistake is what matters the most.

We are little baby humans making our way through life and learning as we go. It's time to drop the heavy weight of self-judgment. It's only hurting you and perpetuating your disempowered cycle. Learn to be gentle with yourself as you make your way through life. Give yourself grace for doing the best you can and forgive yourself quickly when you've done wrong. It is solid to make amends and request forgiveness of those you've offended, but **it's not their forgiveness that lets you off the hook, it is your own.** This is how you fill your worthiness cup and reset your foundation!

Tenet Two—Compassion and Acceptance of Self

Remember you've been criticizing yourself for years
and that hasn't worked. Try giving yourself
compassion and see what happens.

~ Louise Hay

Many of us are kind and compassionate to others, yet we're ruthless and cruel to ourselves. We judge and criticize ourselves for not being *who* we perceive we should be, *where* we think we should be in life, or for not being better in some area. We have little patience and understanding for our shortcomings and have a generally negative view of self. We beat ourselves up for our failures and feel humiliated and ashamed for not doing what we perceive as "better."

We cannot fill our worthiness cups when we criticize and judge ourselves. **Breaking this habit is paramount to curing our inner shame.** This self-love tenet is powerful and will require conscious effort when you first start to practice. But with time and consistency, it can become your default thinking. Most of our mental activity is ingrained or on autopilot. Remember, where your attention goes, energy flows. With consistent effort, you will rewire your brain to think of yourself in a kinder, more supportive way.

Many of us are unconscious of the judgments we have about ourselves. We tend to only notice judgments coming from others. Then we're offended and point the finger at them as the cause of our suffering. But are they really the cause? Interestingly, no. The judgments we have about ourselves are the cause. No one can shame us where we're not already ashamed. Their judgments simply touch what is already in place.

When coaching or mentoring people, I share stories about my history that some might perceive as shameful or embarrassing. If I were secretly judging myself, I wouldn't be able to share so openly. I'd project my self-judgment onto others and hold back out of fear. I'm able to openly share because I have completely accepted my history. I know any disempowered choice I made in the past was an indicator of where I was and I'm no longer there. Because I've done (and continue to do) my self-healing work, I don't project that others will judge me. Furthermore, I'm less attached if they do because I know it's only a reflection of what's going on inside of them. We can't stop people from judging us. This is true. People see people through their own filters. Some see us clearly and others not so much. We cannot control how others see us, but we *can heal* whether or not their judgments hurt us.

This self-love tenet involves learning to maintain perspective when we fail at things important to us or function from our lower selves. It means becoming our own sanctuaries when we feel lost or imperfect. The feelings created from self-criticism are often amplified by ruminating on our hurtful thoughts and emotions. We'll continue to attract more of the same to us unless we apply our focus and energy in an improved way.

A large part of this principle requires seeing ourselves from a broader human experience rather than viewing ourselves as separate and alone. We are never separated from God, so we cannot be separated from each other. To view yourself as separate is to see yourself as "special." **No one holds the title of "special" in any positive or negative way because we're all created equal.** To condemn ourselves is to condemn our soul brothers and sisters too. We are all one. We all chose to come here to learn. We are all imperfect and fallible and we must learn to treat ourselves with kindness and compassion as we navigate this sometimes-tumultuous experience.

Self-compassion and acceptance are defined as an individual's welcoming of their attributes, positive or negative. It's about coming into agreement that you are whole and perfect, quirks and all. **At any given time, we are exactly where we're supposed to be.** There is no rule book about how this life is supposed to look for each of us. The only rules or guidelines are self-imposed. Sure, someone may have judged you first, but you chose to adopt their judgment and make it your own. Give yourself permission to be exactly where you're at without criticism and judgment. Lovingly accept your perceived personality flaws, as they are part of who you are.

You can change a behavior you don't like—that's the cool thing about being human—but resist the urge to feel that the entirety of who you are is based on a few flaws. We all have limitations and shortcomings. We can't not; we are an imperfect species! Be warm and understanding when you're going through a hard time and learn to be the gentle voice that says, "You're okay and everything is going to be okay."

Some people fear that self-compassion is a form of self-pity. This couldn't be more untrue. Self-pity denotes feeling sorry for oneself. It's staying stuck in victim mode. Self-compassion validates our feelings and allows us to be where we are *without* judgment. Much like forgiveness, compassion is understanding we're doing the best we can in any given moment. This gives us permission to be quirky and flawed and still be okay!

Others have said that self-compassion is a form of enabling. Again, those are two different energies. Enabling contributes to the continuation of maladaptive behavior. Enabling is about weakness. Self-compassion is about giving ourselves grace while taking responsibility for where we're at and seeking a solution. It's high vibrational energy that, when applied, will promote healthier behavior. If you check in with yourself, you'll notice self-pity and self-enabling feel daunting, constricting, and weak. In contrast, self-compassion feels light, expansive, and powerful.

Self-compassion and acceptance include mindfulness of where we're at without beating ourselves up for it. The energy is soft, pliable, and provides a safe space for our psyche while we're working through something. It's about becoming the supportive observer of your experience rather than the judge and jury. People Pleasers are typically deeply understanding people. This self-love tenet turns that understanding energy toward yourself. Learn to treat yourself the way you'd treat a dear friend or small child. This is how you fill your worthiness cup and reset your foundation!

A moment of self-compassion can change your entire day. A string of such moments can change the course of your life.

~Christopher Germer

Tenet Three—Respect and Protect Self

Respect yourself. Respect your own inner voice and follow it.

~ Osho

As People Pleasers we tend to put ourselves last, or at least somewhere near the bottom of our priority lists. Many of us were programmed by our families or cultures to ignore our needs and focus on pleasing others instead. At times, our hidden shame and unworthiness have driven us to put others' wants, needs, and feelings above our own in the hopes of gaining their acceptance. We've spent decades lighting ourselves on fire to keep others warm. We've disrespected and dishonored ourselves in the name of being nice or getting approval. The problem is that the body always follows the mind. When we disrespect ourselves, we're telling ourselves (the mind) we're not valuable or important. This programming has us behaving (the body) in ways that promote disempowered patterns. Additionally, dishonoring ourselves makes us easy to guilt and manipulate, which perpetuates lopsided and dysfunctional relationships.

Self-love is about learning to respect and honor our sacred selves by learning to prioritize and protect our minds, bodies, and spirits from anything that depletes our energy or lowers our vibrations. It means putting your oxygen mask on **first** before attending to others. You can't help anyone if you're a fraction of your whole self. A fraction of something will never deliver what the whole can!

Allow me to clarify that "protection" does not imply building a wall around your heart. A wall may keep bad people out, but it keeps good people out as well. Imagine your sacred self as a succulent vegetable garden. Critters love vegetable gardens and can destroy one overnight. If a wall were erected on all sides of the garden, it would keep the critters out. But it would also keep out the sunlight and rain—two vital elements needed for a garden to thrive. A better form of protection is a mesh-type structure that allows the good to come in while keeping away the bad. This is what self-respect and protection look like.

> **Checking in with yourself energetically, emotionally, and physically helps you recognize when you need something different than what is happening right now.**

Assuming others know what you need is a set-up for disappointment and drama. No one knows you the way you do. You are the only person who knows...

...what is acceptable to you and what is not.

...exactly what you want and don't want to experience.

...what energy lifts you and what drains you.

...when you're being harmed and when you're not.

...what feels good to you and what does not.

You're the one responsible for protecting your sacred self and teaching others how to respect you. **It is your responsibility to treat yourself so well that others will have no choice but to do the same.** Relying on others to know what we need or how to treat us is futile and powerless. We cannot control what comes to us, but we can control what we allow to continue. If something harms or drains us, rather than promotes or fills us, we must do what we need to do to respect and protect ourselves above all else.

We are the elite guardians of our minds, bodies, and spirits.
It is our duty to become our own best friends,
advocates, and protectors.

Some people claim they can't make their well-being a priority because they have people or fur babies depending on them or have a demanding career. I understand completely, as I've experienced all these scenarios myself. Self-priority *is not* about disregarding our responsibilities. It's about becoming aware of what *we need* to feel good and supporting it the best we can. Responsibilities and self-priority can beautifully coexist together. It's not necessary to replace one with the other. It's about reducing our over-accommodation of others and becoming more accommodating of self.

Many of us were taught to be nice, not rock the boat, and for gosh sake never make others uncomfortable! I remember the first time (but not the last) I got this message. On my tenth birthday, my mother took me and some friends to play miniature golf. I am petite in stature, so I didn't often win at sports because I wasn't very strong. But this time I was winning! After sinking a difficult putt, I jumped and cheered! Instead of high-fiving and congratulating me, my sweet mother leaned over and quietly spoke into my ear, "Sweetpea, let someone else win because it's your birthday." I remember my confusion. *What? Why? Others beat me all the time. Why can't I win this time? Shouldn't I win on my birthday? Why do I need to let others win because it's my birthday?* I respected and loved my mother, so I did what she asked. I remember feeling so defeated that I didn't even finish the game. I don't condemn my mother for this. She was raised in an environment where women were to be seen, not heard, blend into the background, and make everyone happy. She was only teaching me what she'd been taught, but the negative message—*don't be the shiny one; let others shine first*—stuck for decades.

Respecting and protecting your sacred self may feel awkward at first because it's new. Don't misinterpret this feeling of awkwardness to mean it's wrong. Everything new feels strange until we become better at it. Remember the first time you rode a bike, tried a new recipe, started a new job, or learned a new language? Totally awkward, right? But over time you mastered the skill, and it became part of you. The same concept holds true here.

Respecting and protecting yourself requires creating space before you reply or act. I call it "Practicing the Pause." Pausing affords us time to process before knee-jerk responding with pleasing or any other disempowered behavior. By asking yourself a series of questions (listed below) and answering them honestly and authentically, you give yourself the opportunity to connect with your needs first. Soon enough, thoughtful replies that honor yourself will become your autopilot. No longer will you be at the mercy of those around you because you'll become your own guardian.

Below is a sample list of healthy questions to ask yourself throughout the day that promotes respecting and protecting you. But certainly, don't limit yourself to only these. Come up with your own unique, personal list that supports you and your lifestyle.

Do I want to do what I'm asked to do?

Does this feel good to me?

Do I feel safe doing this?

Is this going to serve me?

Do I have time for this?

How will I feel after doing this?

Is there something I need to do for myself first?

What do *I* need right now?

Will I dishonor/disrespect myself by saying yes?

Is this urgent or can it wait?

Am I enjoying this?

Is this adding or subtracting from my life?

Is guilt pushing me?

This list pertains to any noun (person, place, or thing) we allow into our energetic field—the media we consume, the movies we watch, the places we visit, the food we eat, the drinks we drink, the relationships we keep and so on. The idea is to not become selfish, but to become **centered in self** by knowing what keeps your vibration high!

The ironic and amazing news is that when we're better guardians of our sacred selves, we become cleaner versions of our authentic selves. **Read that again.** We become a more balanced version of who we are. This higher version of self will soon be reflected to you from the outside world. Practicing mindfulness around the nouns you allow into your life tells your inner child they are your priority and you've got their back no matter what.

Respect yourself and others will respect you.

~ Confucius

I understand it can feel scary to make this shift initially. Your old habitual ego-controlled wiring may kick up a fuss. Rest assured, as you practice consistently those fears will diminish. Resist the urge to feel guilty. That's simply ego trying to keep you from healing. Take it slow and easy. Remember, all things rooted in Love serve everyone involved. The more you practice, the easier it becomes. The key is to keep checking in with yourself. Your body and emotional guidance system will alert you to where your energy is depleted, when you're disrespected, or when you're not taking good care of yourself. Be gentle with yourself. You are learning a new method of operation and it may take a minute. This is how you fill your worthiness cup and reset your foundation!

They cannot take away our self-respect
if we don't give it to them.

~ Mahatma Gandhi

Tenet Four—Supportive and Loving Self-Talk

The beliefs you hold, and the words you speak that begin with I
AM, are the energy of creation. This is your greatest power.

~ Howard Falco

Have you ever taken a moment to listen to how you speak to yourself? Many of us have not, yet it's the predominant voice we act from. Repeated thoughts create our beliefs, and our beliefs create our realities. Since the body (actions) always follows the mind (thoughts), we act according to what we think and believe. Since we've never thought to question this voice, we continue to act from old "not good enough" tapes repeating in our brains. If we want a different experience in life, we must become mindful of what we're thinking and believing about ourselves. In Chapter Three, I spoke about reframing our false beliefs. This self-love practice is an extension of that. It's becoming mindful and present with the words you speak over yourself.

When I first became aware of how I spoke to myself, I was astounded. It was nothing short of bullying. I constantly belittled myself and told myself where I fell short. I felt so sad. I couldn't believe how terribly I was treating another human being. There's no way I'd say such demeaning words to someone else, yet here I was saying them to myself.

Consider what happens when someone gets bullied. They shrink, hide, and become a shell of who they once were. They don't trust easily and they're desperate for someone to love, approve of, and accept them. No wonder I'd accepted the unacceptable in relationships, didn't trust myself and was weak with my boundaries. I didn't stand a chance against the onslaught of nasty things I was saying to myself. **We cannot be empowered when we're bashing ourselves.** Period. Bullying has no place on the healing journey.

The key to this tenet is to become super mindful of your inner dialogue. Are you supportive and kind to yourself or are you mean and abusive? I remember a time my friend was talking horrifically about herself. I said to her, "Please stop talking that way about my friend. No one is allowed to talk about my friends that way." She stopped and stared at me. I followed with, "Would you talk to me that way?" She gave me an emphatic, "No way!" I then said, "Then why are you talking to yourself that way?"

One time while stepping out of the shower, I saw myself in the mirror and began to judge myself. I felt myself constricting and wanting to hide from the world. Since I'd become aware of my self-talk, I caught it right away. I spoke back to myself with kindness and love. *Are you kidding? You look fantastic for your age! Look at that amazing body that carried three children! And those feet that have moved you through life. And that skin that's protected you!* I then hugged myself and thanked my body for always being with me and housing my soul in this life. My heart opened, my head lifted, and I no longer felt like hiding.

There's something I've learned on this journey: we can either attack ourselves or we can support ourselves. It's our free will to decide, but it's a decision not to take lightly. The former keeps us small and constricted, while the latter builds and expands us. An empowered person knows which one will contribute to our ultimate healing and which one will not. It's our job to care for ourselves in the best possible manner. This includes monitoring and reframing our inner dialogues. It is a crucial mission and one we must take seriously if we want to raise our vibrations and experience the abundance this life has to offer.

Each time you notice yourself speaking about yourself with negativity or cruelty, catch it and turn it around to a more positive and truer statement. Refer to Byron Katie's four questions and turnaround statement in Chapter Three if you have trouble reframing on the fly. With dedication to the practice, it will get easier and become natural to you.

Reframing Inner Dialogue Examples:

No one likes what I say. People don't listen to me.

I am articulate and entertaining when I speak. People enjoy what I have to say.

I'm fat and ugly (or scrawny and small). No man/woman will ever want me.

I am beautiful and desirable just as I am.

I'm inadequate and will never reach my goals.

I am fully equipped and capable of achieving anything I desire.

I don't matter. No one cares about me.

I am surrounded by people who care. I matter to many.

The positive, reframed statements might feel like lies at first. You may have practiced your old beliefs for so long that they appear real. But they're not. They're only lies constructed from the ego to keep you small. Positive, uplifting statements are always rooted in Love, and Love is the ultimate truth. Even if you can't see it yet, continue to practice loving kindness to yourself. Eventually, you'll retrain your brain to see yourself and others through a completely different lens. This will contribute to improving your self-worth and ultimately draw better experiences to you! The Universe will have no choice but to match your improved vibration with improved experiences.

I was a hairstylist for 29 years. I began when I was 21 years old making me the youngest among my coworkers. Needless to say, near the end of my career I was one of the oldest of my coworkers. Every day I overheard my younger coworkers receiving compliments. I told myself no one gave me compliments because I was old and unattractive, that my ship had sailed, and those days were over. Yikes! Mean! Mean! Mean!

This belief was causing me to suffer, so one morning I decided to play with reframing it. While I was getting ready for work, I told myself how beautiful I am, how awesome my hair is, how great I look for my age, and so forth. I didn't just say the words, I *felt* them. I repeated the statements until my resistance decreased. Then I dropped it and carried on with my morning routine. I kid you not, I wasn't ten feet into the salon door that morning when a coworker said to me, "I love your hair! You have the best hair. You're so pretty." I thanked her and continued on. Five minutes later, another coworker approached me and gave me another compliment. Ten minutes later, another one! By the third compliment, I literally laughed out loud. The poor woman looked at me quizzically. I quickly collected myself and thanked her.

This improved experience didn't happen because I suddenly became young and gorgeous overnight. It was because my internal dialogue shifted and altered my energetic frequency, thus attracting an improved experience to me. It's that simple, folks! The only difficulty I have experienced with this process is learning to ignore the screaming maniac ego trying to tell me otherwise. However, with consistent practice, the ego becomes weaker and much easier to override. I encourage you to keep at it even if it feels incorrect or challenging. Don't quit five minutes before your miracle occurs!

Here's another fun example. When I started public speaking, I was fearful I didn't speak clearly or articulately enough. This belief made me over-the-top nervous anytime I was going to make a video or speak publicly. So, I turned my inner dialogue into positive, supportive statements. I told myself *I am easy to understand, people love to listen to me, and my words are impactful.* And voila! It wasn't long before many people started saying those *exact* things to me. This reframing process is sometimes referred to as using "positive affirmations." You can refer to it any way you choose. The key is to locate your attack thoughts and become intentional about turning them into supportive and encouraging words.

This is a powerful self-love principle. It fills our worthiness cups quickly and sets the foundation for how we allow others to speak to us. When we speak with respect and kindness to ourselves, we're less likely to allow others to speak poorly to us. **You are a sacred and beautiful soul.** No one gets to talk badly about you, not even yourself. Your sacred self deserves to be cherished and honored at all times, even when you make mistakes. There are no words to describe (believe me, I've tried many times) how quickly your confidence and energy elevate when you become your own cheerleader and best friend. Don't beat yourself up if you stumble – practice self-compassion instead. Simply pick yourself up, forgive yourself, and commit to doing better. If improved beliefs alone can lift your vibration, can you imagine what practicing all five self-love tenets will do?

I'm tearing up and cheering anticipating what is coming for you in the future! You are the authority of your life, beloved soul sibling! You get to choose how you are treated by setting the precedent with how you treat yourself. This is how you fill your worthiness cup and reset your foundation!

Tenet Five—Caring for Self

Self-care is not self-indulgence, it is self-preservation.

~ Audre Lorde

Lately, I've noticed evolving definitions regarding the words "self-love" and "self-care." Both are powerful words but hold completely different connotations. Rather than explaining what they are not, I will explain what they are. As described earlier in this chapter, **self-love** is giving to self all things of God/Love. It is a whole unit that is composed of five elements. 1.) Forgiveness and Grace 2.) Compassion and Acceptance 3.) Respect and Protection 4.) Loving Self-Talk and 5.) Caring for Self.

Self-care is a tenet of self-love. It represents attending to your mental, emotional, and physical body with intentional actions that support your ability to thrive in life.

For example:

Eating quality foods

Healthy expression of emotions

Drinking plenty of water

Getting great sleep

Taking alone time

Praying/Communicating with Source

Meditating

Exercising

Getting massages

Eliminating or greatly reducing drug or alcohol consumption

Consuming inspirational material

Spending time in nature

Taking soothing baths

When caring for a small child, a quality caregiver will be attentive to what the child needs for optimal health and wellness. They will provide an environment that prioritizes the child's mental, emotional, and physical health. Babies and young children alert us through their behaviors when they require something to support their well-being. A conscious caregiver will come to understand their signs and signals to fulfill their needs.

When my children were young, I paid close attention to their moods and behaviors and became adept at caring for them. I came to understand that their cries had different tones, volume levels, and intensities. Each cry meant something different. One cry meant hunger, another meant tiredness. Others signaled fear, not feeling well, or a dirty diaper. I also studied their mood changes and energetic levels. By coming to understand their signals I became proficient at keeping them peaceful and happy.

I remember dining at a restaurant one evening when my daughter was around a year old. About ten minutes after we were seated, she started crying. I tried the usual things to calm her, but none of them worked. This cry felt different somehow. I used a side door of the restaurant to take her outside. This door led to a parking lot, so I sat on a cement parking stopper thinking we'd be there awhile. The minute I sat down, she stopped crying. We remained outside for about five minutes before rejoining the family. She wasn't in her highchair thirty seconds before she started wailing again. I was confused as to what was going on, so I took her back outside. The second we were out the door, she stopped crying again. After walking in and out of the restaurant several times, I realized how loud it was inside. It dawned on me that the din of the restaurant might be too much for her.

Still carrying her, I tried an experiment. I stepped just outside the door and her crying stopped. I stepped just inside the door and her crying started. I did this several times and the results were always the same. Her crying was like flipping a light switch. At this point, I was fairly certain it was the noisy restaurant causing her distress. Needless to say, I stayed outside with her and ate my meal at home.

As time went on, I noticed she reacted to other high-volume things, like vacuuming. She'd cover her ears and say, "Too loud, Mommie, too loud!" She'd also cover her ears when I turned on the bathtub faucet. It turns out my daughter is a Highly Sensitive Person (much like her mama), and excessively loud environments are overwhelming to her. From that point forward, I knew she needed low-volume environments to thrive.

I share this story to demonstrate what it takes to be a good caregiver of others and of self. Much like the way we learn to interpret the "tells" of a small child, we must learn to interpret our own. If we've been out of touch with our emotions and body sensations, we might not know what we need immediately. No worries! You'll come to know yourself well when you dedicate yourself to this practice. When we're children it is our caregivers' responsibility to give us what we need, but when we become adults, it becomes our responsibility. Some of us were well cared for as children and some of us were not. Oftentimes children whose needs were not met grow into adults who don't know how to meet their own needs. The good news is, unlike deciphering a baby's signals, learning to decipher your own is much easier.

Physical body sensations and your emotional guidance system will alert you when something is out of balance.

For example, stress and overwhelm may alert you to take some time off, get out in nature, or practice presence or meditation. An upset stomach or diarrhea may alert you to clean up your diet, decrease alcohol consumption, or reduce stress. Low energy may alert you to go to bed earlier, eat higher quality foods, or exercise. Sore neck muscles may alert you to take an Epsom salt bath or get a massage. Feeling cranky and irritable may alert you to take a nap or spend some time alone. The better you come to know your emotional and physical tells, the better able you'll be to care for yourself. With time and commitment, you'll become skilled at knowing exactly what you need and when you need it. The key is to follow through!

Note: Self-care does not replace treatment for medical conditions. Always consult your health care provider if you're experiencing problematic mental or physical symptoms.

Make it your daily practice to check in with yourself periodically by asking, *What do I need right now?* Be honest with yourself. Then ask yourself, *Can I meet this need now?* If yes, great, if not, tell yourself you'll tend to this need as soon as possible. Following through is just as important, if not more so, than the discovery. This is where you reprogram little You to know they are important and your priority.

You may already know some areas you could take better care of yourself. Take a moment to formulate a list of non-negotiable self-care areas you're willing to commit to right now. These are areas you're not willing to compromise. It doesn't have to be an extensive list to be effective. Here's a sampling of my non-negotiables. These are things I strive to achieve every day.

Eat organic, high-quality food. No preservatives or imitation sugar.

Get eight or more hours of sleep each night.

Drink mostly water and unsweetened green tea.

Limit time with negative people.

Refrain from watching movies or shows that include abuse or torture.

Zero to little caffeine intake.

Move my body in an active way.

The above list was formulated over several years as I became aware of what it takes for me to feel good every day. The concept of "self-care" wasn't as widespread in the past as it is now. Therefore, I didn't realize until much later how powerful having a list like this is. I also didn't stop at just this list. Additional self-care methods arise spontaneously as I check in with myself throughout the day. Sometimes I need a nap or have a random craving for vegetables. Sometimes I need to meditate or read inspirational literature. Sometimes I need to take a walk alone or sing at the top of my lungs. The key is to observe (not judge) what arises for you and follow through as much as possible. Just like caring for a small child, be willing to try different methods to see what gives you optimal results. Don't get discouraged if a recommendation from another person doesn't fit for you. We're all different and require different things to feel balanced. Investigate and play with as many methods as possible to discover your best self-care plan.

Self-care not only keeps the mind, body, and spirit balanced, it teaches little You that they are valuable, and you matter! When little You knows you're important, big You will demonstrate that in the world. It also teaches those around you that your well-being is a priority too.

Fun Fact: Since coming to know how important it is for me to maintain my well-being, it's become my practice to ask my loved ones what they need when I notice their mood or energy change. I don't ask what I can do for them, but what they need to do for themselves. Many times, we know what we need but we're afraid to do it for fear of pushback or disapproval. Permitting your people to care for themselves provides a better environment for everyone involved. Grounded and balanced individuals generally contribute to higher functioning relationships.

Our lives become enriched when we honor the requests of our mental, emotional, and physical bodies.

**Self-care is not selfish; it is necessary to move
from surviving to thriving!**

Allow your self-care practice to take precedence and become part of your daily life. As your vibration rises, you become clearer, balanced, and happier. Not only will you benefit, but the world around you will also benefit. This is how you fill your worthiness cup and reset your foundation!

Life wasn't meant to be about suffering. God didn't come to a slow roll and throw us off the bus while waving and shouting, "Good luck! See ya after a while!" God didn't leave us alone with only our tiny human minds to guide us. No. No. No. The power of God/Love has never left us and never will. We didn't separate from God; we came here with God. You are all things good and Holy. You are a child of God; you are a spark of Divine Energy. You are whole and perfect just the way you are. God doesn't make mistakes. You are a warm-hearted, compassionate, and generous Earth angel. It's time to treat yourself with the same respect, compassion, and acceptance you give to others.

Reclaiming your power requires healing the wounds acquired along your life's journey and dismantling the disempowered behaviors that came with them. It's giving yourself what was missing in your childhood by re-parenting that little girl or boy within. Become your most trusted and valued protector and guardian. We can't change our pasts, but we *can have* an empowered future. We do this by returning to the unconditional love within that is our birthright.

Intrinsic Values Worksheet

Affectionate: touching or holding in a loving way

Ambitious: determined to achieve success

Caring & Considerate: thinking of others

✓ Child of God: Divinity resides within you

Communicative: sharing ideas, thoughts, and plans verbally

Creative: using imagination for original ideas and works of art

Enthusiastic: excited about life

Faithful: remaining loyal and steadfast

Forgiving: willingness to release past betrayals

Funny: causing people to laugh

Gentle: kind and tender

Good listener: paying attention when others speak

Kind: thoughtful and caring

Loyal: giving or showing firm and consistent support

Motivating: stimulating interest or enthusiasm in others

Open-hearted: openly expressing warm and kind feelings

Pleasant: easy to be around

Polite: exhibiting good manners

Resilient: able to withstand or recover quickly

Responsibility Taker: recognizing and owning behavior

Seeker: willing to search for answers

Self-Starter: motivating self to explore new endeavors

Sincere: being totally honest

Tenacious: displaying persistence to achieve a goal

Thoughtful: thinking things over

Vulnerable: willing to share deep thoughts and feelings

Chapter Seven

Setting Healthy Boundaries— Teaching Others How to Treat You

Remember, you're the most important person in your life. Until we begin to value ourselves enough to meet our own needs, we can't expect others around us to do it.
Take it one day at a time.

~ Louise Hay

Who knew that setting healthy boundaries could be so complicated? Not this girl. I assumed setting limits with people who were treating me poorly would be easy. I'd speak the boundary, they'd follow the instruction, and all would be well. But that didn't happen. I found myself having to repeat my boundaries many times and received pushback and arguments instead of compliance. It seemed every time I spoke up about poor treatment, it was turned around on me. I've been called controlling and a know-it-all, told I was PMS-ing, and was even labeled a narcissist once.

I remember back in high school when my best friend (who I'd known since birth) and my boyfriend cheated on me, people acted like I was out of line for not wanting to be around them. *Wait a minute, they betrayed me. Why was I the bad guy?* Another time I kindly mentioned to a longtime girlfriend that she had no-showed her last three hair appointments with me, and it was creating space in my schedule that I couldn't fill at the last minute. And *she* got upset with *me.* What's worse, we never spoke again. *What the bleep?* I didn't get it. If someone called me out on rude or disrespectful behavior, I apologized and did my very best to never do it again. Why wasn't I receiving the same? I'm sure many of you can relate to these examples and so many more. As Byron Katie says, "There are no new stories." The characters and scenarios might change, but the feelings are the same.

Boundaries can be more complex than we were taught to believe. Therefore, my intention with this chapter is to help clear up any misconceptions you might have regarding what boundaries are, how to set them with intention, what bolsters our practice, and what to do if your boundary is not heeded.

What are Boundaries?

Boundaries (noun) [plural]:
unofficial rules about what should not be done:

limits that define acceptable behavior.

Boundaries are the way we communicate through words and actions what is unacceptable to us. They set proper limits with others that clearly convey what we are not willing to put up with and what we will not allow into our lives and energy.

Boundaries are designed to protect and support our sacred selves.

They are the sentries of our minds, bodies, and spirits. Without healthy boundaries, we run the risk of feeling disrespected, depleted, taken advantage of, or intruded upon. Those feelings can lead to anger, resentment, burnout, low self-esteem, or anxiety and depression. Not only are those dense emotional spaces to function in, but they can also contribute to the disconnection and breakdown of our relationships. Without boundaries, relationships are superficial and flimsy because people are dancing around the truth rather than engaging with it. The problem is that without addressing our feelings and establishing appropriate limits, our relationships cannot grow and flourish. Well-placed boundaries serve to fortify the structures of our relationships because both parties are treated in respectful and loving ways.

All relationships are designed to show us ourselves. They are classrooms to learn in. They reflect and project what is happening in our inner worlds—where we are empowered and where we are not. When two personalities join in a relationship (romantic or platonic), each party brings a set of ideologies, fears, belief systems, programmed habits, behaviors, and patterns. Each shows up in a way that communicates their values, emotional wounds, and where they're at on their respective spiritual journeys. Each participant has an opportunity to determine what aspects of their behavior are acceptable and which ones are not.

Allow me to be radically clear here. Limits are not about trying to change a person into your idea of perfection or to manipulate them into giving you what you want. They're also not about building a fortress around your heart and expecting someone to break it down. Boundaries are based on the desire to be treated with respect and kindness and a keen understanding that it is our duty to teach others how to do so.

Setting treatment parameters with others is where the rubber hits the road with reclaiming our personal power. This is where owning our true worth really happens.

Healthy limits are self-love in action.

It is our responsibility as recovering People Pleasers to treat ourselves well and to teach others how to do the same. Because many of us have histories of being disrespected, dishonored, and unprotected, it can feel commonplace when we're treated as such. In the beginning, it can be difficult to discern the line between what is okay and what is not because we are used to certain treatment. Therefore, self-love is paramount for our people pleasing recovery. Self-love does more than simply reset our foundations. It shows us (for perhaps the first time) what it feels like to be respected and honored. When we're kind and respectful to ourselves, it becomes blatantly obvious when others are not. We become clear-sighted and resolute where we were once wishy-washy and unsure.

We cannot experience a loving and respectful relationship if we're complaining about others' behaviors but are unwilling to do something about it. Healthy limitations transmit to the world that you know who you are and what you deserve. They demonstrate you're willing to do what it takes to be treated well. Every day we have opportunities to teach people how to treat us. Assuming others "should know" what is intolerable sets the relationship up for breakdown. When we communicate where our lines are, our people don't have to guess about what's required to be with us. Additionally, we're not carrying extra emotional weight for not standing up for and taking care of ourselves.

Which Comes First—Self-Love or Boundaries?

Any place we are not empowered, someone will overpower.

~ Dr. John Demartini

Not long ago, I had a conversation with a gentleman who's a dating coach. He mentioned he often tells his clients to set boundaries, inferring that it's easy. I explained to him that it's not that easy for some people. Speaking up about our limits is one thing but holding them can be challenging. If we don't have a secure foundation (self-worth) in place before setting a limitation we run the risk of folding, for several reasons. One, we're more worried about the other person's perception of us than our self-respect. Two, if the boundary was set from anger or frustration, our strength diminishes as the emotion fades. And three, we're more afraid of being alone than being treated appropriately.

He respectfully pushed back and said that humans learn through repetition and the more you do something the easier it gets, just like learning to tie your shoes. I agreed that repetition does indeed make things easier, although learning to tie a shoe doesn't involve emotional "risk" (real or perceived). Boundaries can be quite scary and intimidating at first. Although there are people who find boundary setting easy, there's a whole slew of people who find it challenging or even impossible.

Many of us realize a need for boundaries but are unable to set them for fear of the consequences that may arise from them. Or we set flimsy boundaries hoping they'll "get it" so we don't look like the bad guy. This is where self-love makes all the difference. A person with a healthy level of personal value will naturally have an easier time respecting and protecting themselves.

**Healthy boundaries are an organic
response to self-worth.**

We still may not enjoy setting boundaries, but we can no longer allow bad behaviors to go unaddressed. However, what the gentleman was suggesting is also true. Science supports that we get better at something the more we practice it. The repetition of new thoughts and behaviors forms new neural pathways in our brains. This is called learning. Neural pathways are the configuration of connections among the neurons (brain cells) in your brain. You can think of them as patterns that represent any simple thought such as a banana or a more complex thought like intuition.

Every thought we have is a result of a neural pathway. Some neural pathways are well formed and referred to as dominant, whereas others are new or fragile and referred to as lesser. The more we practice or repeat something, the more dominant the pathway becomes in our thinking, language, and behavior. Think back to my previous example of spelling and vocabulary words in grade school. We learned them by restating them many times until eventually, they stuck. The same concept applies here. We can become proficient at setting boundaries the more we practice them.

So, what comes first—self-love or boundaries? Well, it depends where you are on your journey. Remember, recovering People Pleasers are on a spectrum. If you're already good at setting boundaries, your self-love practice will fortify it. If you've never been good at them, your self-love practice will foster it. So, the answer is both. Setting boundaries becomes easier the better we love ourselves **and** the more we practice them. It's not important to discern what comes first, nor is it necessary to know where you fall on the spectrum. It's only important to start working on them. Like the beloved Louise Hay said in the opening quote, "Take it one day at a time."

Boundaries Serve Both People

When we start setting boundaries within our established relationships, people will likely resist. After all, we've trained them that their needs and wants come before ours and we haven't required them to act any differently. Since they're used to getting their way with us, they'll likely fight back when we no longer allow it. Their fight, however, is often not only about them not getting their way. Boundaries also shine a light on the boundary receivers' unhealed places—their dependencies, selfishness, fears, or controlling behaviors. Your boundary can spring their ego into action which can ignite intense emotions. These emotions can result in behaviors such as, but not limited to, denial, defense, gaslighting, or emotional outbursts.

Taking responsibility for our behaviors is an act of our Higher Selves. It is rooted in Love, which ultimately means death to the ego. It will do everything in its power to prove you wrong so it can preserve itself. Since many people commune with the ego more so than their Higher Selves, they may fight back fiercely. Understanding what happens in these types of situations gave me the strength to hold my line(s) because I knew their attacks were simply their ego fighting for its life and it had nothing to do with the validity of my boundary.

Setting boundaries (especially with our loved ones) can seem intimidating at first. The fear of losing their affection or love, hurting their feelings, or making them angry can feel quite daunting. As People Pleasers we often care about others' feelings over our own. We justify or make excuses for their behaviors because we fear potential fallout. We may subconsciously feel undeserving of better treatment or fear being alone. Instead of risking upsetting or losing someone in our lives, we upset and lose ourselves instead. We become fractured versions of who we are and then wonder why we keep experiencing lopsided and painful relationships and feel unfulfilled.

I've always had high standards for myself. I've always wanted to be the best daughter, sister, friend, mother, and partner I could be. I'm a lover and a nurturer, after all. When I originally received pushback for my boundaries, I'd fold because I felt like I was doing something wrong. Then I learned something powerful.

**Anything rooted in Love is always Right—
even when it's love of self!**

Setting healthy boundaries is an example of God working through me. Since pure God Love always works **for the highest good of all concerned,** I realized that healthy boundaries serve both parties.

**A firm, well-set boundary gives the other person
the opportunity to discover and heal disowned
aspects of themselves.**

Both parties win when we are willing to set healthy limits. We get to be treated better and they get to grow! How exciting is that?! Now, I'm not implying this is the sole reason to set boundaries. It's not our job to keep tabs on other peoples' growth—that's God's business. However, it might help to know that a boundary rooted in the Love of self is showing love to your person too! Our job is to love ourselves to the best of our abilities and let the rest fall into place. You will likely discover your firm boundary was the best thing to happen to your relationship.

Below are a few self-affirming statements to utilize if you receive pushback or feel weak and tempted to renege on your boundary.

- Others' denial or deflection does not mean my boundary is wrong.

- I cannot control other people's behaviors. I can only control my own.

- I am not responsible for other people's feelings or lives. They are responsible for their own.

- I am worthy of respect and honor.

- My time is valuable. I get to choose the best use of my time.

- My job is to take care of myself first so I can take great care of others.

- It is 100% acceptable to support my needs and desires.

- I am happier and more balanced when I take care of myself.

- Taking care of myself is a gift to me and those around me.

Here's the scoop: most often we need to set boundaries with those we love and who love us the most. Although it's new to us and may feel awkward at first, it's important to know that your loved ones don't want to lose you either. Many people aren't willing to look at their behaviors until they have a good reason to do so. Your boundary could be that reason! Be brave. Be consistent. Don't give up because you receive pushback. Stay focused on respecting and honoring yourself and allow others to make the necessary corrections to do the same.

Action Boundaries—When Words Aren't Working

If they don't believe what we say, they'll have to believe what we do.

~Kristen Brown

As mentioned earlier, I was under the impression that boundaries were one and done. I thought others would conform to treating me better if I simply asked. That was not the case at all. I began to realize that it wasn't only my words that mattered, but my actions as well. I learned the long way that if my spoken requests weren't working, I needed to follow up with action. I call these "action boundaries."

A while back a person in my life was chronically negative. I'm not blind to the chaos of the world, but I don't spend a lot of time focusing on it. Not only was this person negative, but their tone and volume were unpleasant to listen to. I tried many times to bring something positive to the conversations or change the subject. It didn't work. I tried telling them I like seeing the good in the world, not wallowing in the ugly. That didn't work. I told them with calm assertiveness that I wasn't going to participate in those low vibration conversations anymore. And that didn't work. Each time I tried setting a boundary, they'd get upset with me and say I was selfish for not listening to them. I explained that I enjoy talking to them, but it's my responsibility to protect my energy and these conversations were low vibe and draining. Still, nothing changed.

Knowing I can only control *my part of the equation,* I told them I was going to remove myself the next time they were on a negative rampage. I had to excuse myself from approximately ten conversations before they got the message and stopped plopping their doodoo on my doorstep. But here's the best part! That person eventually stopped focusing on all that's wrong with the world and morphed into a more positive and appreciative person. Not only did our relationship become more peaceful, but they became one of my favorite people to hang out with. My healthy boundary became a catalyst for their positive change.

In this story, it's clear that words were not working. It wasn't until I removed myself from the situation that they finally got it. That's what action boundaries can do for us. **Many times, people won't connect with our words, but they'll connect with our actions.** The key is to be willing to do whatever it takes to respect and protect yourself *even* if that means removing yourself from their proximity. And... this is important... the calmer and more assertive we are, the better they'll respond.

I remember many times sharing my feelings with my first husband regarding his disrespect and dishonor towards me, to no avail. I figured I wasn't clear enough, so I'd talk and talk and talk about it until I was blue in the face. I tried everything—crying, begging, pleading, threatening—and nothing changed. It was maddening to me that no matter how upset I was, he didn't seem to care. In hindsight, but without regret, I see how I could've handled it differently. I say "without regret" because I believe everything in life is purposeful and it's not serving our highest good to regret what we didn't know how to do. What I didn't realize is that no matter how shitty he was to me, he still got the "whole" of me. This wasn't only true for him, but for all my past relationships. I never changed my behavior in response to their behavior with an action that the person couldn't ignore or deny was happening. This action may have promoted them feeling the loss of my energy and therefore be willing to do whatever it took to get it back.

Many times, we try using threats as a means of getting someone to treat us better. In my experience, threats never worked. Not once. They might have scared someone for a minute but when I failed to follow through, they stopped fearing them. What got the best results was performing an action I knew I could follow through with. By repeating that action, which usually involved removing my energy from them in some capacity, they'd realize they couldn't have me under the conditions they were posing. If respect, honor, and kindness aren't part of the equation, I pull myself out of it until further notice.

Appropriate action boundaries are specific to each situation. I can't begin to list all the ways to apply an action boundary; however, it might help to ask yourself some questions to decide the best action to choose.

What does this person love getting from me? Time, attention, etcetera?

What do they expect from me? To always be there or to put them first?

Where would they feel the loss of my presence/energy the most?

Find a way to pull your energy back from them so they can get a glimpse of not having the entirety of you. Then follow through with that action until you see true ownership or a willingness to make a change. I implore you not to think of this as manipulation. Manipulation is schemed control rooted in selfishness. Action boundaries are rooted in self-respect. Think of it as removing a privilege from someone who's abusing or exploiting it. Your presence and attention are another person's privilege. If they refuse to treat you respectfully, they don't get the whole of you.

Speak Up Sooner

You better know that in the end, it's better to say too much
than never to say what you need to say again.

~ John Mayer

I have a long fuse. I can put up with a lot for a long time. I used to think it was a superpower until I realized I was doing myself a disservice. Like a burning fuse connected to a bomb, once my fuse was burned up, I'd explode. Although everything I said was truthful, my tone and volume overshadowed my words, and the focus would turn to *my* behavior. It didn't matter that they were treating me poorly or that I'd requested 187 times for them to stop doing the thing. All that ceased to exist the second I lost it. *Oh man, I used to hate that so much.* I used to be stuck in the unfairness of it all, but I've since learned that I can live as a victim, or I can rise above it. Each situation in life provides us an opportunity to learn and grow. This scenario taught me something powerful—if I want to be heard, I need to speak in a calm, assertive way long before reaching my saturation point.

I taught myself not to deny, excuse, or ignore the niggles of disrespect I was picking up on. I learned to address behaviors as soon as possible in real time. Sometimes it was in the moment and sometimes it meant waiting until we were in a private space. It's important to take into consideration who's around and what is happening when addressing certain things. I'm not about public shaming people—that's just lowering our vibrations to match theirs. If you can't address the issue privately while in public, it's likely best to wait until you have privacy. Obnoxiously calling someone out in public might be appropriate on a rare occasion. But when it's used to shame, you're out of alignment with your Higher Self and will likely contribute to the problem, not the solution.

I've been told many times throughout my life I'm a patient person. For the most part, I believe that I am. Yet waiting endlessly to speak up regarding bad treatment and calling it "patience" was misleading.

I was a doormat. I saw the behavior, I felt the pain, and I shrugged it off as insignificant or too small to address. I wanted to be seen as easy going and fun to be around and calling out poor treatment all the time negated the persona I was trying to fill. But here's the irony: when I started addressing issues before they got too big, I was *naturally* more easy-going and fun to be around because I wasn't carrying around extra emotional baggage. These types of paradoxes come up all time on our healing journeys. Watch for them. They're fascinating.

Now, speaking up sooner doesn't mean pointing out every little thing someone does. It does not mean we become behavior police. We can have healthy boundaries and still be the understanding and loving people we've always been. But when you start to feel prickly about someone's actions, that's your cue to pause and investigate. For example, if a person is venting to me about an event in their life and somehow their frustration turns towards me, I might ask myself questions like this:

Are they going through something rough right now?

Is their behavior directed at me?

Is this how they always treat me?

Am I being disrespected in this process?

Considering the facts, do I need to set a boundary?

I have no problem holding space for someone struggling. I value emotions and I'm all about the healthy expression of them. I also know how much can be gained through our challenges. But if someone's bad mood turns into an attack on me, that's my cue to speak up.

I use a calm, assertive tone and volume and say something like this, "Hey [insert their pet name], I know you're really struggling right now and I'm here for you. I love you and I want to help. I'm not the one you're upset with so please stop directing this at me." Then I repeat it as often as necessary. I'm also willing to remove myself if the behavior continues. This method has yielded amazing results in my life. Notice I didn't attack or belittle the person. I spoke only about the respect I require when conversing with me. By practicing this method, I noticed how they began practicing this in their own circles. (Another example of how boundaries serve both parties.) That's a win-win if you ask me!

Note: It's important to mention that children and teens haven't learned how to effectively process their emotions and it's highly beneficial to use caution and care to not shut them down when they're attempting to share with you. It's crucial to provide our children with safe spaces to share with us. If we overcompensate with restrictions, we could shut them down for good. Be mindful of where your child is at emotionally. A raised voice doesn't necessarily mean they're being disrespectful. If your situation does require a boundary, be sure to set it in a calm, assertive tone and return to them when they've calmed down.

Giving Grace to the Boundary Receiver

This one's a biggie. I invite you to open your heart and mind to what I'll be sharing in this section. It might appear like I'm going against what I've said so far but hang in there while I unpack this concept.

It's important to understand that when we start setting boundaries, especially if we haven't in the past, we're changing the rules for people. They've been dealing with us in a certain construct and suddenly we're telling them it's not okay anymore. When I got serious about protecting my sacred self, I had some work to do with a few people in my life. My lack of speaking up had permitted them to continue acting a certain way. Most human behavior is on autopilot, which means it happens without conscious thought. So, it's going to take some time for our people to become aware of their behaviors and make necessary adjustments. This is where giving grace to our boundary receivers is beneficial. In the same way we extend grace to ourselves while we're learning something new, it's advantageous to extend grace to others while they're learning something new. With this, we set the stage for them to *want* to change. If we're constantly focusing on where they're falling short, they might wonder why they're even bothering.

Disclaimer: This doesn't imply we stay with abusive people in the name of grace. Verbal, emotional, and physical abuse most often escalates into something bigger. It's imperative to have a hard line regarding abusive behavior and to get yourself and those dependent on you to safety immediately. This section only refers to typical, non-violent relationships where we are retraining a person to treat us better.

After My Tsunami, my three children and I lived with my mother and stepfather. It was a loving environment and I'll be forever grateful for their kindness and generosity. My mother pretty much became my co-parent. I often told her she was the best husband I'd ever had! (Yet she was still the adoring grandmama and liked to spoil her grandbabies.) My two oldest children were in high school and fairly independent, so she didn't "help" with them. But my third baby was quite young and since my mother was retired, she cared for her while I worked. The two of them were tight and spent considerable time together. (My daughter's memories with her "Papa"—that's what she calls my mom—are very dear to her.) When I asked my mom if their time together was too much, she'd always reply with, "She's my love and my light. She gives me life." She never strayed from that statement. Not once. However, the spoiling was real.

When we moved into their house, my little one was four years old and ate only fruits and veggies. It was by her choice. While most kids beg for candy at the grocery store, she'd snag random veggies out of the produce section and munch away while we shopped. One time she ate three small tangerines off our tree, rinds and all! Another time she ate an unpeeled banana from the end up. (I checked with the pediatrician about her eating the peels of fruit and he assured me that if it didn't create a problem with her digestion, it was perfectly fine.) This child had zero desire for sugar when we moved into my mom's house, but over time that's all she wanted. (My mom had a sweet tooth the size of Australia and I'm sure the two of them partied it up when I was away.)

My daughter also became addicted to getting new items. She'd persistently ask for toys and trinkets. Alarm bells were ringing for me. I'm all for buying things for my kids and allowing treats, but I'm also about a healthy diet, delayed gratification, and teaching them how to earn things.

One Friday after picking up my daughter from school, she was bugging me about getting her a specific toy. I told her no. I was going to attend a three-day conference that weekend, so I asked my mom to please not buy her the toy. I explained how she was getting spoiled with toys and sugar, and we needed to reign this in as a team. She agreed and I trusted she would do the right thing. When I got home on Sunday, my little one ran up to me to show me what Papa got her. It was the toy she'd requested on Friday. I smiled and acted happy for her, but I was fuming on the inside. I calmly asked my mom why she went against my instructions. She shrugged and dejectedly said, "I don't know." She went on to say it wasn't the right thing to do, she apologized, and said she'd do better.

My mom was always a generous person. It gave her great joy to give to others. If it wasn't for the fact my father was so frugal when we were growing up, I'm certain she'd have spoiled me and my brothers too. She bought the toy out of love, but also because she had difficulty saying no to people. I knew that about her, but I also knew it wasn't good for "our" child. Not only was my daughter getting spoiled, but she was getting teased at school for her weight gain. I knew my mom understood my boundary, but I also knew she'd be changing a lifetime habit. I held my line, and I gave her grace while she learned. She did her best to get my permission before buying my daughter a toy or giving her sugar. She wasn't 100% great at it, but she showed definite improvement.

Not all people are capable of immediate change. We're all works in progress. However, if we're seeing a significant change in the right direction, this indicates our person is aware and working on it. Give them grace while they learn. A great way to identify when someone is in the process of breaking a pattern is if the negative behavior diminishes or becomes less frequent. If you notice a significant change in your receiver, be sure to share your appreciation with them. Most people bloom under conditions of appreciation and validation. Since it feels good, it encourages them to keep at it. Seeing consistent progress over perfection is a great sign your person is trying to respect your line. Most often, it's only a matter of time before it'll stop for good.

If your person constantly ignores your boundaries, keeps treating you poorly, tells you you're crazy or selfish, or continues to gaslight you, it's safe to say they've no intention of changing a thing. Do your best to not get sucked in by charming words no matter how much they say they're "trying" or attempt to sweet talk you.

Words mean nothing; actions mean everything.

Zero movement in the right direction means it's time for an action boundary. Pull your energy back until they are ready to honor your line. If nothing changes, it's time to consider if you want to keep investing your precious energy on them.

All situations in our lives happen *for* us, not *to* us. It's how we show up to them that matters. There are no hard and fast rules for how to handle the multitude of personalities and situations we each deal with.

It's up to us to love ourselves well and make solid decisions that support our well-being and the well-being of those dependent on us.

Sometimes our loved ones want to please us, but they stumble in the process. Extending grace while they learn is an act of Love and could be exactly what your person needs to rally up for the win.

Boundaries in Hindsight

It's never too late to start. It's always too late to wait.

~ Jeff Olson

Have you ever wished you'd said something different after stepping away from a conversation or argument? Did you become clearer about things after you had time to process the interaction? This section is about what to do post-situation. It's about giving yourself permission to revisit conversations and scenarios at a later date—no matter how much time has passed. I call this "reserving the right to revisit this later." Just because you didn't say the thing you wished you'd said in the moment does not mean you cannot go back to it later. Conversations and topics are not always over once the subject changes. Many times, while thinking about things in hindsight, we realize we were too firm, not firm enough, or our perspective of the situation changes. It is healthy relationship protocol to revisit conversations after they're over if it's in a productive way.

I once had a friend who had an unhealthy relationship with alcohol. She'd drink to the point of "shitty," as we liked to call it. She was a beautiful girl and had an amazing figure, yet she had very little self-worth. She thought her body was her value and would go home almost every weekend with a random guy she'd picked up from a bar or club. When I talked to her about the risk factors of this behavior, she'd shrug me off like it was no big deal.

One Sunday morning while I was enjoying quality time with my kiddos, she called to ask if I could pick her up at a hotel and take her to her car. She was my best friend so of course, I said yes. She told me she'd left the club with not one, but two random guys and they got a hotel room for the night. (The guys did not know each other.) When I picked her up, she told me she didn't know where she'd parked her car. We drove to all the places she'd been the previous night before we finally found it.

At the time, I was the "ICE" (In Case of Emergency) contact in her phone's contact list. After dropping her off, I became more and more annoyed. For one thing, I was a busy single mother, and I was tired of being her babysitter and rescuer when she consumed too much alcohol. And two, I'd already been concerned about her reckless behavior, but this was over the top. Two random dudes in a secluded hotel room and she couldn't even remember where she parked her car? Come on! It had reached a new level of concern for me. I needed to say something, but I didn't know what.

I processed through my feelings for a few days or so, then decided to write her a letter. I shared how important she was to me and how her excessive drinking and reckless behavior affected me. I told her each time she went out, I feared getting a call from the police requesting to identify a female body found murdered and dumped in a ditch. I also told her if this behavior continued that she'd need to remove me as her ICE.

We worked together in a salon and our stations were right next to each other. At the end of my workday, I loitered about waiting for her to go to the back room for something. When she finally did, I placed the letter on her station and hightailed it out the door. I was filled with fear and anxiety because I'd never set a boundary with her before and frankly, she was a moody thing. I expected to get the silent treatment at work the next day, but that didn't happen. She called me on her way home that same evening. She apologized and told me she understood because she'd had to write a similar letter to a family member.

Sometimes it's favorable to wait before addressing a situation. Permit yourself to process first, then decide how you'd like to handle it. Be strong and don't shy away if someone tries to bully you into silence by saying something like, "Oh God, you're bringing this up again?" or "Why can't you just drop it?" or my favorite, "That's in the past!" There's no time limit to when you're allowed to speak up about something, no matter how far in the past it happened or how much they try to dissuade you.

Being excellent guardians of our mental and emotional health will require doing hard things.

Reserve the right to revisit any situation that feels incomplete to you. If the situation or behavior is affecting your well-being or someone dependent on you, it is your right to speak up at any point.

The Two Biggest Boundary Mistakes

It probably goes without saying that the biggest boundary mistake we can make is not setting one in the first place. The second mistake is inconsistency. Since People Pleasers tend to choose cuddles and kisses over confrontation, it's easy to let things go, become complacent, and hope for the best. Sometimes this works and sometimes not so much. I'll share a little story that highlights this in a playful way.

Although my family of origin had a dog growing up, I was too little to be involved in caring for or training her. In 2005 when I got my first dog as an adult, I had zero clue how to be a dog owner. To be honest (and I know this might sound ridiculous), I didn't know they required training (insert eyeroll). I naively thought that some dogs were just good and some not so much. I bought my little doggo, Robbie, at a pet store. He was a Bichon Frise. Please don't hate on me for the pet store purchase—at the time I knew nothing about puppy mills. At eight weeks old, this little ball of fluffy white hair came to live with us. I researched potty and kennel training, but that was the extent of it. I took him outside once an hour the first couple of days and pointed at the ground while repeating, "go potty." He'd then go potty. By day two, he began alerting us by standing next to the back door. And that was that. He was potty trained. Bada bing, bada boom.

One day we were working in the front yard. Robbie was under a year old. I saw him making his way toward the sidewalk that ran alongside the street. I called to him **one time** and said, "Robbie, no, no. No street." And can you believe that boy never once walked into the street without us for the rest of his life? I can't make this up! As most dogs do, he barked incessantly when people came to the front door. It took maybe five times of me sternly saying, "no bark" before he stopped doing it completely. (I don't mind alert barking, but I'm not a fan of incessant barking.) He also didn't chew on things, get into trash cans, or sneak random snacks off plates left unattended. He was so easy, I figured I had this dog training thing in the bag.

One very sad day, Robbie passed away. The pain was excruciating. I'll never forget my sweet, sweet boy. Robbie had been gone for a couple of years when my children started pushing for another dog. Enter Wesley! We acquired Wesley from a rescue agency. He, along with his mama and seven siblings, was brought down from northern Arizona to a shelter. My goal was to choose an easy, friendly dog just like my Robs. I told my kids that the first pup that consistently approached us each time we visited would be ours. Wesley was always the first to greet us and smother us with the sweetest puppy kisses. We chose him as our new family member.

Not long after having him home, reality hit. To say that Wesley was difficult to train is an understatement. He chewed on everything, he wouldn't follow commands, and he peed everywhere. He jumped all over everyone and scratched them with his claws. He constantly nipped at and put his mouth on us, sometimes cutting us with his sharp puppy teeth. He wasn't aggressive, but it certainly hurt. And the crazy-scary part was, he was obsessed with swallowing ped socks and hair scrunchies whole. *What the heck was happening here?!*

I hired two different trainers and spent endless hours binging puppy training videos. I learned great tips from all, but there was one running theme through all the information I was consuming: consistency. I couldn't let anything slide. The second I did, he'd go back to his old ways. Before y'all start wondering if we were missing something, I promise you we spent hundreds of dollars on chew toys to keep him busy. (He annihilated chew toys in less than 5 minutes. We graduated to the heavy-duty ones made from fire hose material and he'd chew through those in less than two hours.) We played with him a lot and took him on long walks and car rides to burn energy and keep him entertained. He wasn't unruly because we neglected him. He was just... well... Wesley! I'm happy to report that he is now the best boy ever. He follows my commands, loves people, and is truly a joyful part of our family. Consistency was the key.

I share this story because humans are much like dogs. Some humans are simply easier to "train" than others. Some are like Robbie—they learn quickly and don't require much boundary maintenance. Others are like Wesley and require consistent boundary maintenance to get the results we want. Neither pup is better than the other—they are both special and unique in their own ways and loved equally. Robbie learned commands easier, but he was too small to hike with me. Wesley can hike for miles but was more challenging to train. It's not fair to classify dogs (or humans) as good or bad regarding how compliant they are. We're all vastly different and learn at different rates. When we understand that everyone is wired differently and some humans require more "training" than others, we set ourselves up for success. The good news is that most of us learn well when faced with consistency and repetition.

When teaching others how to treat us (or training a dog or raising kids), being inattentive and lackadaisical will not yield the results we want. If you truly want to be treated with respect and kindness, you must be willing to do whatever it takes to achieve it. **Stay consistent with your practice.** Those who love you and don't want to lose you will do whatever it takes to keep you. Those who are selfish and in it just to take from you will likely move on. Either way, you win!

An empowered person understands that boundaries say: *I matter. My opinions matter. My needs matter. My well-being matters. To be with me is to honor and respect me as I do myself. And I, too, will equally honor and respect you.* You are the only one who can break your doormat behaviors and teach others what's required to be your friend or lover. It's all about creating relationships that honor and respect the person you are by unapologetically communicating what is unacceptable through your words and actions.

Chapter Eight

Connect with Your Divinity

*The greatest comfort in life is having a close
relationship with God.*

~ David O. McKay

It was somewhere in the early morning hours—what most refer to as the middle of the night. I couldn't sleep. I was lying in bed wide awake with anxiety coursing through my body. Everything that made me feel secure in the world was washed away in one gigantic wave. My second husband had left me and my three children (the youngest his biological child) for another woman. Shockingly, I was okay with him leaving as the previous year was a virtual hell. I chose to view it as God doing for me what I'd been unwilling to do for myself. What scared me the most was that I retired from my 19-year hairstyling career and clientele to manage the responsibilities of home and family. My former husband was an international pilot who flew a private jet for a Nigerian oil magnate. His work required him to be gone for five to six weeks at a time and I was stressed and exhausted from handling everything myself. Retiring felt like a solid decision.

Hairstyling is a client-building career. It typically takes one to three years to build a clientele in a healthy economy. This event was taking place during America's biggest economic downturn since the great depression. To say it'd take years to rebuild my clientele was an understatement. Additionally, hairstyling is commission-based at first and requires sitting for endless hours, day in and day out, waiting for walk-ins. I had no other skills, and a minimum wage job wouldn't scratch the surface of our financial needs. With no substantial means of income, I faced being homeless with three children in tow. I remember thinking, *How did I get here? I've worked since I was fifteen years old, I've never missed a bill, and have an excellent credit rating.* All that I had worked for in my life was erased by the selfish acts of another. I was living in a state of sheer terror. My children are my greatest priority, and I was about to fail them.

Instead of lying in bed tossing and turning, I decided to go downstairs. I wasn't five feet off the last step when my intestines began to rumble, and I was instantly nauseous. I felt like I was going to vomit and have diarrhea at the same time. I wasn't sure I'd make it to the bathroom without a projectile mess along the way. My ears began ringing loudly and my vision narrowed. I dropped to my knees so I wouldn't pass out, and I attempted to crawl to the bathroom. The tile floor felt like a million tiny knives thrusting into my kneecaps. The pain was excruciating. There was no way I could stand the tortuous 30-foot crawl to the bathroom. I found a patch of carpet nearby and flopped down onto my back. As I lay there, I thought, *Well, this must be bottom. It can't get any worse than this. I'm destitute and about to be homeless. I'm all alone, my kids are upstairs asleep, I have no phone nearby and I'm about to vomit and shit all over my carpet. Yay me.* For some reason, I started laughing. I laughed as if I'd heard the most amazing joke. I could feel my body jiggling from the laughter, but I could hear nothing above the deafening ringing.

My financial situation was disastrous, there was no denying that. There was nothing I could do to stop my fate, and no one could fix this for me. As I lay there resigned to whatever mess was about to happen, I remembered God. *Wait a minute... I'm not alone... there's God... God is supposed to help us through difficult times.* I'd always believed in a Higher Power, an invisible energy that is all loving and good. I mean, God was my playmate in childhood when none of my friends could play. *Why hadn't I thought of this sooner?* In that sacred moment, I let go of trying to control and humbly invited God to help me. Within what appeared like seconds, my ears stopped ringing, my guts stopped clenching and my equilibrium corrected itself. It was as if none of those symptoms had existed. I stood upright, walked up the stairs, crawled into bed, and fell into a deep slumber.

Calming the Nervous System

You cannot always control what goes on outside, but
you can always control what goes on inside.

~ Wayne Dyer

Upon awakening the next day, I recalled my "physical nervous breakdown." I knew I had to figure out how to calm my anxiety because I didn't want that to happen again. I remembered my days of practicing Kundalini yoga. After each class I experienced a feeling of total peace and clarity—as if no fear existed. I wanted that feeling back. Kundalini yoga primarily focuses on breathwork, so I committed myself to a breathwork practice. Every day I'd lay on the floor of my bedroom and perform deep breathing techniques—sometimes for two hours. I wouldn't allow myself to get up until my heart stopped pounding, I could inhale and exhale deeply, and I felt more relaxed.

I'm also an avid hiker, so I'd get myself on the mountain as often as possible. I'd focus on my steps and my breathing while absorbing the serenity of nature. After each intentional practice, my fear and anxiety were considerably reduced. Initially, this semi-tranquil state lasted less than an hour, but I could feel the payoff of my efforts, so I kept soldiering on.

My former husband and I were going through the divorce process and not surprisingly, he was fighting hard. It wasn't my intention to screw my soon-to-be ex over or to seek vengeance. That's not the person I am. I wanted what was appropriate and fair to support me and my children while I rebuilt my career and life. I made my intention clear to God. My mantra/prayer all day, every day was: *Thank you, God, for the best possible outcome for all concerned.* I repeated this mantra each time fear (the need to control) arose within me and I continued my calming practices. Almost immediately, I started receiving random spiritual messages and signs. I could tell they were from God by the way they felt. There was a gentle "clicking" sensation accompanied by a feeling of neutrality and peace. I interpreted these signs as God's response to my plea, and I took a leap of faith and followed them. Little by little the pieces of my life fell masterfully into place with precision so flawlessly crafted that it could've only been orchestrated by Divine Intelligence.

Since this experience over a decade ago, I learned that maintaining a calm nervous system and moving energy through the body are two of the most empowered actions we can take. When the brain is stuck on high alert (fear), its only goal is to "survive." Our fight, flight, or freeze response is activated and we either attack, run, or hide. In this state, stress hormones like cortisol and adrenaline are released, our blood pressure and heart rates increase, and we breathe faster. Blood moves away from our hearts and into our limbs, preparing us to run for our lives. When this "survival mode" activates, our world becomes very narrow and constricted. Our creative brains shut down and won't allow for "flow" because our only goal is to survive. This is why it can be difficult to make decisions or be creative when we are riddled with panic and anxiety. Interestingly, the brain does not know the difference between a physical threat or an emotional one, so it reacts the same for both.

In today's world, the most common threats we encounter are emotional. They are activated through external stimuli such as dysfunctional relationships, dramatic or traumatic events, the news, other negative media, and our programmed ways of thinking and believing. These stimuli create thoughts. Repeated thoughts create beliefs, and both create heavy emotions. The heavy emotions activate more supporting thoughts and beliefs, which create more heavy emotions, and so on. Thus, a cycle of fear ensues. We can easily get stuck in this "survival mode" unless or until we do something to interrupt it. We can't receive our divine guidance and follow our intuition when we're stuck in fear. For optimal mind–body balance and connection to our Spirit, we must calm our nervous systems.

Over the last decade, I've acquired a cache of tools and techniques to assist me in calming my mind and body. The more benefits I receive, the more I realize how integral this practice is to my self-care regime. Below is a list of the tools and techniques I've collected over the years. I decide which one(s) to implement by asking myself higher self, *What tool(s) would best serve me right now?* I allow for the inspired feeling to land and then I follow it.

Meditation—guided, not guided, and walking

Emotional Freedom Technique—aka Tapping

Listening to binaural beats and other frequency-specified music

Sound healing meditations—I sure love me some gong and crystal bowls!

Nature walking

Practicing presence

Alone time

Yoga

Breathwork

Questioning my limiting beliefs

Vagus nerve stimulation

Quality time with my pets

Exercise—cardio and strength training

You are not required to use my tools, nor are you limited to them. The journey to reclaiming your power is about **becoming your own authority** and choosing what works for you. Go on the explore, soul sibling! Ask other people what their favorites are, utilize Google, read literature, watch YouTube videos, and listen to podcasts to fill your personalized toolbox.

Intuition—Connecting with Your Inner Guidance

The intuitive mind is a sacred gift, and the rational mind is a faithful servant. We have created a society that honors the servant and has forgotten the gift. We will not solve the problems of the world from the same level of thinking we were at when we created them. More than anything else, this new century demands new thinking. We must change our materially based analyses of the world around us to include broader, more multidimensional perspectives.

~ Albert Einstein

Merriam-Webster's online dictionary describes intuition as *the power or faculty of attaining direct knowledge or cognition without evident rational thought or cognition.* Our intuition arrives through clairvoyance (clear seeing), claircognizance (clear knowing), clairaudience (clear hearing), or clairsentience (clear feeling). Oftentimes we connect with one clair first. Claircognizance was the first to show up for me when *I knew* I was going to win the drawing for "Tweety" the hamster. As I grew, I developed the other remaining three. I now hear, see, and feel messages as well. Although each clair is different, they're always accompanied by the same calm, still, and neutral feeling.

Many of us don't recognize our intuitive "hits" due to their subtle natures, so we pass them off as insignificant. Yet, in hindsight, we'll say things like, *I knew I shouldn't have done that*, *I had a feeling that would happen*, or *something was telling me not to go there.* These occurrences are reminders you are connected to a power that literally holds galaxies together. It knows the entire picture and exactly how to orchestrate the manifestations of your desires. We can become masterful at following our divine guidance when we attune ourselves to receiving it.

I included intuition in this book because learning to trust our divine guidance is an act of true empowerment.

Trusting and following our intuition is the ultimate demonstration of being our own authority.

The messages we receive will always be timely and specific to our lives, situations, and next best steps. It is information designed to serve *our* distinct life paths and it will always, 100% of the time, be correct. There is no greater, more serving, and spot-on guidance than that which comes from God. We are not alone here. We are connected to a field of infinite intelligence that vastly exceeds our minuscule understanding. This field is loving and wants us to thrive! Our job is to tune in and become aware of the messages it's sending so we can move purposefully and powerfully through life.

Many people say they don't receive intuitive hits and I respectfully disagree. No one is exempt from spiritual guidance—it is built into the architecture of our being. Those who think they aren't intuitive are simply not practiced in receiving guidance. We often hear about "women's intuition," but not of man's intuition. This is misleading. All human beings are connected to Source and can receive guidance. Think of male detectives on real-life crime shows who have "hunches" or "sinking feelings." That's intuition disguised under different terminology. Unfortunately, many men have not been given the grace to feel, be emotional, or trust their inner guidance. They've been told it's girly or bad or wrong, so they've learned to mostly rely on the rational mind or "faithful servant," as Einstein so eloquently stated in this chapter's opening quote. If you're someone who feels disconnected from your intuition as an adult, it doesn't mean you can't reconnect to it. We came to this dimension with this ability. It's not gone, it's simply buried under your analysis, fear, and desire to control.

Intuition is one of my all-time favorite topics because (1.) it demonstrates the equality among us as God's children, (2.) it's warned me of impending danger multiple times, and (3.) it has guided me to victory more times than I can count.

When we heal our self-worth, we're better able to follow our intuition because we don't allow others to talk us out of it.

We're more focused on living our best lives than on getting approval from others. These days if I receive an intuitive hit, I'm unshakeable. No one can convince me that it's wrong. I know when God is speaking to me, and I know to trust it fully.

This was the case when *I knew* a certain person was having a medical issue with their brain. I desperately urged the person's loved ones to take them to the doctor immediately, but no one listened. I was growing increasingly more agitated by the day because *I knew* something bad was coming and still, no one took me seriously. I felt as helpless as watching a car crash about to happen and not being able to stop it. About two weeks later, the person had a massive stroke and died a short time later. I'll admit I was super angry and carried that around for a few weeks until the person came to me in a vision and said, "Don't be angry. There was nothing you could do. It was my time to go. Thank you for always being so nice to me." Even when we get hits about others, it doesn't mean we can interrupt their life paths. Sometimes the messages are simply a "heads up" about what's to come.

About a year ago, I received a random hit about a certain person. I knew this person was not who they claimed to be. I only told one other person about it. The hit was so "out there," I hardly believed it myself. Two weeks after I received the hit, the truth came out. It was exactly as it was given to me—the person was a fraud. They had completely lied about their identity. At that moment, the "friendship" we had was finished. Fascinatingly, even after others learned the truth, several made excuses for the person and continued to be their friend. Just because you receive an intuitive hit doesn't mean others are going to appreciate it or trust it as you do. Everyone has the power to make their own choices and decisions; it is their free will. Our intuitive guidance is intended to assist *our* lives specifically, not others. Unless of course, we're doing some type of intuitive reading for someone else.

I invite you to get deeply connected to your Higher Power and your intuition despite any pushback or resistance you receive from others. **Learn to trust yourself and Source in an unshakeable way.** However, be mindful to know the difference between stubbornness and intuition. Stubbornness is rooted in ego and a need to feel powerful. It feels tense and constricting. Intuition is rooted in Love and feels neutral, light, and expansive even when it's a warning. For example, one morning upon waking up, I heard a sweet melody accompanied by lyrics in my head. The lyrics were, "It's my time to leave you." I told my friend I intuitively knew one of my parents was going to die and they should not try talking me out of it. My friend stared at me unblinking in shock but stayed silent. My beloved mama transitioned five days later.

When we know what we know because we know it and don't allow others to make us second guess ourselves, it's an indicator we're healing our people pleasing patterns. We're no longer relying on the opinions or approval of others to validate our thoughts, feelings, and experiences. This doesn't mean we have to stop sharing our concerns, issues, and stories with others. Sharing what's happening in our world can often help us gain clarity. It simply means we trust God/Source/ Universe and Self above all else and we make solid choices and decisions in communion with it.

The more you act on your intuition fearlessly, the more your intuition will serve you. Intuition is the ear of the soul.

~ Neale Donald Walsch

The Magic of Surrender

*When we surrender to God, we surrender to something bigger
than ourselves—to a universe that knows what It's doing. When
we stop trying to control events, they fall into a natural order,
an order that works. We're at rest while a power much
greater than our own takes over, and it does a
much better job than we could have done.*

~ Marianne Williamson

One of the most powerful gifts we can give ourselves is the gift of surrender—to let go, let God. When I finally understood I was not alone and the Universe had my back, I was able to settle into the unknown more comfortably. It was a tremendous relief to know I did not have to brave this life alone. I know there is no better place for my worries than to hand them over to a power that sees the bigger picture and knows exactly how to move the pieces of my life into alignment with victory. Human beings want to control because we fear the unknown. We think we need to put our grubby little hands on everything for it to work out. But...

What if God knows better than you?

What if there is a better way?

What if your "control" is only adding chaos to what God is trying to clear up?

The best control we can ever have is surrender. Our free will allows us to choose between deciding from the mind or deciding with God. When

I learned that there is so much in my life that is better off in the hands of God, it permitted me to stop "doing" so much and relax more into "being." I also learned to check in with my higher self/inner guidance before making any decisions.

To live in the illusion we can control everything only promotes and prolongs our suffering. We tend to let God handle our less significant worries, but the ones we are deeply attached to or believe are more important, we want to control ourselves. *A Course in Miracles* states, "There is no order of difficulty for miracles." This means there is no hierarchy of what's important to God. God is equipped to handle big things just as readily as small things. We can fret and worry and try to manipulate situations, but that's likely to prolong the blessings that God is trying to bestow upon us.

Eight months after our separation, my former husband and I appeared for a court hearing to determine the monetary issues of our divorce. I had never testified in court and had no idea what to expect. Since my family's financial livelihood and future were at stake, my fearful mind took over. The closer I got to the courthouse, the higher my anxiety rose. Sitting outside the courtroom, I leaned my head against the wall and began to meditate. I focused on my breath while repeating a surrender mantra. I was astounded by how calm and centered I was as I entered the stand and prepared for questioning. My former husband's attorney was aggressive, to say the least, and treated me as if I was on trial for a heinous crime. He did his very best to rock me, but I was unshakeable. I didn't have to fake my peace or "act" in any way because I had surrendered.

Thirty days after our last hearing, the judge's orders arrived in the mail. I had to read the document three times before it finally sunk in. I was granted all I had requested and more. My children and I were going to be okay. *Thank you for your guidance, God, thank you.*

> **Surrender is not giving up on a situation—it is giving it over. It is not "thinking" our way through life but acting from divine inspiration.**

Surrender means getting out of our way and letting God lead us. So many times, I went through life believing if I thought hard enough, I'd come up with the solution. Although the analytical mind is powerful and purposeful, sometimes the answer is outside our limited views. This doesn't imply the solution is difficult—in fact, it's almost always quite simple. It means we haven't yet learned or practiced it so it's not yet part of our mental processes. We only know what we know, and we'll repeat situations and scenarios until we acquire new information. When we open our hearts to new information and allow God to lead us, life flows more gracefully.

An example of this occurred when a loved one and I had conflicting viewpoints. I was beyond frustrated at their inability to see the big picture. I went for a drive to clear my head and spoke tersely to God. "What do I need to do here?!" Within seconds I heard, "Stop talking." That was not what I was expecting. However, this message was calm, neutral, and felt like what I've come to know as the voice of God. So, I trusted it. To be honest, I felt somewhat giddy because I knew if it came from God, it would help. When I reentered the space with my loved one, I stopped trying to convince them of my viewpoint. I didn't make faces or roll my eyes, I just listened. Instead of trying to be understood, I sought to understand. And soon thereafter, the other person's "fight energy" diminished and a calm, quality conversation ensued.

God does not force, God leads. But only upon our request.

God will not impose on our free will. If we want help, we must ask for it. Then clear the runway for the message to land by opening our hearts and minds to new perspectives. When we surrender how we think things should go and allow the Universe to work its magic, things fall into place better than we could ever imagine. The Universe has the whole picture. It knows when, where, how, and what. Our job is to trust in a superpower far greater than our understanding to lead us to our next best steps and decisions. The following is my favorite Surrender Mantra when I find myself trying to control something.

God, I'm giving this to you because it is beyond my scope of knowledge, understanding, and skills. I know you see the entire picture. Please guide me. I am open to your wisdom. And so it is. Amen.

Forgiveness of Others

Forgive others not because they deserve forgiveness,
but because you deserve peace.

~ Johnathan Lockwood Huie

Forgiveness does not mean we condone our perpetrators' behaviors. What they did is not okay, and it never will be. It was wrong, it hurt people, and it was damaging. Forgiveness also does not mean you must allow the perpetrator back into your life or that you are required to talk to them again. Martin Luther King Jr. once said, "The Lord never said I had to like my enemies." Amen to that.

Forgiveness is for you, not the other person. Carrying contempt and hatred only darkens your heart, not your perpetrator's. Your unforgiveness does not punish your wrong-doers—it only punishes you. Holding onto hatred, bitterness, and anger does not poison your enemies, it only poisons you. Forgiveness is clearing low vibration energy from the mind, body, and spirit. It is choosing Light over darkness. It is releasing the toxic tie between you and your perpetrator. Forgiveness is duly noting the wrongdoing, releasing the emotional burden of carrying it, then choosing an appropriate action or boundary if needed.

Forgiveness is freedom—freedom to live without added emotional weight, freedom to take our power back and freedom to choose whom we allow in our lives. When we choose forgiveness, we dissolve the emotional links that keep us connected to our offenders. We may not get to see their karma returned, but we can rest knowing God is handling it.

Mohandas Gandhi said, "The weak can never forgive. Forgiveness is the attribute of the strong." Forgiveness is not always easy and may sometimes feel more difficult than holding onto contempt.

It takes fortitude and courage to release the desire to punish our perpetrators and heal ourselves instead.

One might believe that non-forgiveness gives us control or authority over another person's life, or that it holds them accountable for their actions. This is untrue. Our perpetrators will continue to live their lives regardless of whether you've forgiven them or not. I assure you, your wrong doer is not holding themself back because you haven't forgiven them. Unless or until they have a wake-up call, the justifications and lies will continue throughout their lifetime with little or no thought about whether you have forgiven them. In choosing forgiveness, we work toward keeping our hearts open and minds clear to move forward in life unencumbered by emotional baggage regardless of what our perpetrators are doing or thinking.

God's Business

There is no revenge so complete as forgiveness.

~ Josh Billings

The wrongs others commit are God's business, not ours. God knows exactly when we stray and what each of us needs to learn and grow. It is not up to us to play God. We are minute in comparison to the infinite intelligence of the Universe, and we simply do not have the power to handle it. Peace comes when we truly believe God has all situations handled.

Our job is to take care of ourselves the best we can, so we may show up in our lives in the highest possible ways.

Part of excellent self-care is reclaiming our power through the practice of forgiveness. Yet, there is something we can do for our perpetrators. We can send them love so they may be returned to their Right Mind. Some of you might be thinking... *What?! No way!* I completely understand your reaction, and may I gently remind you that is your lower self (ego) keeping you from healing. Thich Nhat Hanh, a Vietnamese Buddhist monk, author, and peace activist, so eloquently stated, "When another person makes you suffer, it is because he suffers deeply within himself, and his suffering is spilling over. He does not need punishment; he needs help. That's the message he is sending."

My former husband and I returned to court two years after our divorce over child custody modifications and his non-compliance to the conditions of our divorce decree. He had not seen or spoken to our daughter in those two years. (He was absent for a total of seven years.) During the months of preparation, I spoke telepathically to him almost every day. Even though I believed his behavior was unethical and difficult to comprehend, I chose to appeal to the glimmer of light I knew was underneath his cloak of wounds. After all, he is still God's child no matter what he's doing.

I said: *I know you love your child, and you know I am taking great care of her. Please open your heart during these proceedings so we may come to a mutually fair agreement so I may take the best care of our little girl in your absence. Please know when you play fair, my stress is decreased and I'm a better mama to her. I know who you are [God's child], and I know the good you are capable of. If/when you are ready, you will be welcomed back into her life. Thank you.*

I even made a social media post asking everyone to "... send love to a person I am currently dealing with who has strayed to the dark side, so he may feel, for at least a moment, the right thing to do." Many people knew my story and could guess who I was talking about. They were also initially shocked at what I was requesting; however, something in their souls understood.

I desire to stay in alignment with the highest possible energy. To keep my hands and heart clean. I can do this by staying as closely aligned with Love as possible. This doesn't mean I don't feel emotions or follow through with action if required. Marianne Williamson once said, "I can forgive you and still sue you." This means I can go higher by understanding that my wrong doers have lost their way **and** I can still take appropriate legal, ethical, or moral action. What they've done is not about me, but about themselves **and** some behaviors have consequences attached even if we've forgiven.

Be "Willing" to Forgive

The willingness to forgive is a sign of spiritual maturity. It is one of the great virtues to which we should all aspire.

~ Gordon B. Hinckley

Forgiveness is about releasing the misdeeds of others to keep ourselves in alignment with Love, or at least be willing to try. After my mother transitioned, my stepsisters pulled some insidious shenanigans—the types of things that leave you standing with your mouth agape. You see them, but you can't believe someone would actually do them. I allowed my emotions because they are natural, and I didn't want to repress them. But every time the topic arose in conversation, I felt instantly enraged. If I'd not experienced the effects of forgiveness in the past, I'm certain I'd have validated my anger and done nothing about it. Although I was justified in my feelings, I knew my non-forgiveness was only hurting me.

I tried my usual forgiveness practice. I thought of my stepsisters as innocent children doing the very best they could, and I did my best to understand *why* they would do something like that. Most often, I feel a slight release at this point, but nothing budged. I tried again... nothing. I was deeply grooved in like a tic on a dog. My ego's desire to be right was strong. *This was my mother! How dare they?! She only ever loved and cared for them!* I realized I was not willing to forgive them at all.

The next day I brought it to God. *God, I am willing to forgive them.* Again, no release. I went deeper. *God, I am willing to be willing to forgive them.* This time I felt something. It was an ever-so-slight release, almost like someone unlocked a door but hadn't yet opened it. I said it again and then one more time. It was slight, but it was more than I'd felt before. I knew I'd broken through. I said, *Thank you, God, for handling this for me* and I moved on. Frankly, I didn't expect much to come from that exchange. Approximately five days later the subject came up and I noticed my intense anger was gone. I looked around for it, but it was not there. What they did was still not okay—it will never be okay—but the all-consuming fire of rage was extinguished. I felt peacefully detached while we discussed the topic.

God can do for us what we cannot do for ourselves. If we are fully willing, God will step in. Sometimes that requires us to be willing to be willing. Or to be willing to be willing to be willing. Use however many "willings" it takes for you to unlock the door for God to enter.

Most of us have heard the phrase "hurt people hurt people." When we've lost conscious contact with who we are, we can inflict damage on others in sometimes catastrophic ways. People become the collateral damage of our unhealed wounds and sometimes we become theirs.

Forgiveness is a shift in perception where we choose to view another's wrongful behavior through spiritual eyes instead of through eyes of judgment, condemnation, and control.

It is about consciously choosing the Higher path as opposed to filling our hearts with darkness like the person who betrayed us. Marianne Williamson states, "[Forgiveness] is converting your thinking to a spiritual perspective. You train your mind to be on the lookout for the blessing or the innocence. People tried to do the right thing. It's more than a paradigm shift—it's more of a worldview shift."

Forgiving others (and ourselves) helps reset our energetic foundations.

I knew I had given enough of my energy toward my stepsisters' betrayal. Continuing to live within the energy of their immoral behavior was only hurting me. It was time to take my power back. If there's one thing I've learned on this spiritual journey, it's that I have a say in what I allow into my energetic space. Others' betrayals may pop in for a visit, but they don't get to set up camp and stay any longer than necessary.

Forgiveness does not go without reward.

It's often a silent reward that manifests in glorious ways that may be undetectable to anyone but us. Our energetic fields clear, our vibrations rise, we make sound decisions, and we become more powerful manifestors. Forgiveness affects our general well-being, our levels of personal peace, and our abilities to navigate life unburdened and free.

The Universe is Abundant

It is our Father's good pleasure to give us His kingdom.

~ Jesus

You can have anything you want. There are no limitations to what you can have in this life. It's all there waiting for you in escrow. One of my coaches once said, "I want it all—love, family, joy, fun, adventure, health, wealth, and career." She said it with such conviction that something shifted deep inside of me. I gave myself permission to want it too **and** I believed it was possible. So many of us play small. We say things to God like, "I *only* want this little thing. That's it. Just give me this one tiny thing and I'll never ask for anything again." Whoa, hold up there now. Do you realize that God wants you to have anything and everything your heart desires? Do you know that those desires are put into your heart *by* God? And that the Universe has an endless stream of abundance for everyone? When you're thinking small, you're only denying your birthright as a unique and brilliant co-creator with the Universe.

A friend of mine once believed she was being humble when she asked God *only* for "a man who is nice to me." Guess what happened?

She got a man who was nice to her BUT he didn't treat her as a priority, he was non-committal, he was emotionally unavailable, and he flirted with other women. So I ask you, does it work to play small? To deny your birthright as a brilliant conscious creator? To create the life of our dreams, we must be willing to know *exactly* what we want to experience and stop doubting that it's possible.

Not long ago, a fellow coach and friend of mine called. He said he wanted to thank me. He explained that he never thought he could have all that he wanted in a romantic relationship. He didn't believe there were many women out there who would jive with his concept of ideal partnering. He went on to say that listening to me repeatedly say that we can have everything and anything we want and by watching my life unfold into all it is, he chose to believe it was true. He made a list of the attributes he wanted in an ideal partner, and he wholeheartedly believed it was possible. He called me to share that he'd met the woman of his dreams! She checked all the boxes of his ideal partner, and he was madly in love. Shifting his perception from lack to abundance removed the blocks for her to come into his life.

Some people choose to be the voyeurs of other people's lives, secretly wishing they could have what others do. But instead of working towards those things, they live vicariously through them. Where do you think the obsession with reality television comes from? If you truly want something, it's time to get to the business of bringing it into your reality. Stop trying to *force* the outcome by feeling desperate for it. If we look closely enough, desperation is rooted in the belief that we cannot be happy until it arrives. This energy works against the manifestations of our desires. The key is to become happy first. Have you ever wanted something so badly and then finally gave up? And when you did, the thing you wanted came magically floating in? That's because your "giving up" released the resistance to its arrival.

When I was 21 years old, I wanted a boyfriend so badly. I was on the mad hunt to have one and it consumed much of my thinking. My desperation drove most of my decisions—what I wore, where I went, who I visited, and so forth. I felt like I had to put myself in the right place at the right time. I felt like I had to do all the work. After months of striving and not getting the results I wanted, I asked myself why I wanted a boyfriend. What did I think that was going to do for me? I realized it wasn't going to do anything for me—I was quite happy being single. So, I dropped the notion altogether.

A week later, the chef from the resort I worked at invited me to an old stagecoach stop that had been converted into an outdoor bar and restaurant with firepits and live music. While waiting in line to buy a beer, I noticed the guy in front of me. I told him he looked familiar, and it turned out we had gone to the same high school. He was an upperclassman I'd seen walking around from time to time. I remember back in high school thinking he was cute. We parted ways after getting our beers and went back to our groups. As I was walking out to leave, I passed his group, gave him a wave, and said goodbye. He waved back and that was that.

The next weekend I attended a "barn dance" to kick off a yearly parade that is held in my hometown. This event hosts popular country music performers and thousands of people attend. While waiting in the girl's restroom line (because there's always a line), I saw him again. This time he was standing with a woman. I gently patted him to get his attention, said hello, and moved on. The following weekend, I was with a friend at another establishment. And guess who was standing at the end of the bar? The same guy! I had not seen this guy since my sophomore year of high school and here he was three weekends in a row. Long story short, he became my first husband.

It's imperative to let go of desperation for our desires to come in. We must have an unshakeable faith that the Universe knows what it's doing. After all, it is powered by an intelligence so magnificent that we cannot possibly understand it. The Universe sees the entire picture, not just the limited view that we have. Consider a beautiful tile mosaic on a large wall. When you press your nose to it, you can only see what's directly in front of you. But when you step back you can see the entire picture. We, as tiny humans, see only the nose-pressing view, but God/Universe sees the whole shebang and knows exactly how to orchestrate life in our favor.

Letting go, however, doesn't mean you can sit on your bum waiting to land the monster music deal, an incredible romantic partner, or your dream job. Manifesting our dreams requires effort, although it must be the right kind of effort delivered to us through inspiration. It's about following what feels right or inspiring to do next—not what we *think* we need to do. Expending tremendous energy just to feel we're "making it happen" often leads to burnout and hopelessness. Some things may take a little longer as you push through your fears, develop parts of yourself that are dormant, or heal in some way. But that doesn't mean you aren't destined for it or allowed to have it. Jack Canfield, author of the widely popular *Chicken Soup for the Soul* series, said, "If you've gotten to the point where you would like to experience something, that means it is possible for you. You just have to get to work at making it happen."

My friend and Law of Attraction expert Andy Dooley often reminds us, "Feelings first, manifestation second." This means aligning with the *feeling* of the wish fulfilled prior to its arrival. Know exactly what you want then feel "as if" you already have it. Take one inspired, intentional step at a time. God/Universe has your best interests at heart and is delighted to help you achieve your dreams. In the meantime, relax and have fun with this simple six step practice.

1.   What do you want?

2.   How will you feel when you have it?

3.   Believe it's 100% possible.

4.   Take inspired steps in that direction.

5.   Continue to feel "as if" you already have it.

6.   Relax and have fun.

Mike Dooley is a New York Times bestselling author, speaker, and widely known for his contributions to Rhonda Byrne's documentary *The Secret.* Years back I subscribed to Mike's daily inspirational messages written from the Universe's perspective. They're called "Notes from the Universe." Upon signing up, the questionnaire asks what you'd like to manifest. I listed three very specific things I wanted. Occasionally, the daily emails are customized to include your specific desires. Last week I received an email that mentioned the three desires I listed. As I read the email, I realized two of the three had manifested and they were biggies! I also know *why* they manifested. I set the intention for the experiences I wanted to have, I made inspired efforts towards achieving them, and I let go of when, where, and how. I kept my "eye on the prize" as I like to say, while never losing faith that it was possible.

Abundance is not something we acquire;
it's something we tune into.

~ Wayne Dyer

One of the biggest hurdles people experience with manifesting is having the belief it's possible. It's not my job to convince you of this, but I am inspired to share this Truth with you so you can investigate deeper for yourself. By fully believing anything is possible, we shift our energetic vibrations into alignment with receiving it. Some things may take a little longer to manifest as we are *prepared* for the receiving of them. For example, I had a deep desire to share my wisdom and knowledge to help people reclaim their power to attract and create amazing relationships, but I had a tremendous fear of public speaking. Internally, I wasn't yet prepared to receive my desire because of the limiting beliefs and fear I had around it. Universe heard my desire and led me by one inspired step after the next. I was first inspired to write a book and build a website and blog—with zero technical skills, I might add. Blogging landed me invitations to write as a guest expert on other websites and forums. During this time, I developed my language and writing skills to convey somewhat complex concepts into easy-to-understand material.

Eventually, writing blogs and articles felt limiting to me; I wanted to connect more intimately with people. This led to the creation of my podcast and later, my YouTube channel. From there I received invitations for live appearances on other content creators' platforms and was offered an amazing opportunity to help launch what is now the fastest-growing social audio app. The culmination of these experiences grew my confidence and shifted my energetic vibration, which aligned me to experiencing the successful career I have today. God/Universe held my hand and walked me to it one step at a time. My only job was to trust and show up.

Just because your dreams haven't yet arrived does not mean you cannot have them. Never fear, God/Universe has heard your request— the moment you ask, the desire is given. Each inspired step God/Universe lays before you is designed to reconnect you with your True Worth so you can become a perfect vibrational match to receiving and achieving all you've ever wanted.

Life doesn't happen *to* us; it happens *for* us. Every experience you have is designed to help you reveal and heal places within you that block you from experiencing your best life. Trust that the Universe is abundant and wants to fulfill all your heart's desires. Paulo Coelho, author of *The Alchemist* said, "When you want something, all the Universe conspires in helping you achieve it." It may not look or go the way you think it should, but trust above anything that Universe/God knows what it's doing.

The fact that you purchased and read this book to the end tells me you're dedicated to reclaiming your personal power. You listened to your inner guidance and followed your inspiration. And if you got from this book what I hoped you would, I am certain you've changed the trajectory of your life toward an empowered future. Well done, soul sibling, well done!

Take it one day, one hour, one minute, or one step at a time, but never lose faith. Be willing and able to become the person who is magnetic to all they desire. Set the intention of what you'd like to experience, show up to your divine guidance, and trust that it's on the way. You are deeply worthy of experiencing mutually loving and respectful relationships and anything else you desire. You always have been.

It is your birthright. ♡

READER BONUS!

Because you are embarking on the courageous journey of self-discovery, healing and reclaiming your personal power, we're extending an exclusive offer to the readers of

The Recovering People Pleaser

We want to help jumpstart your process by offering you **three guided self-love meditations**, written and recorded by Kristen Brown.

Whether you are new to meditation or a pro, these guided meditations will help you replace self-doubt and unworthiness with self-value and confidence to foster a more empowered state of being.

Cheers to you, beloved soul sibling! For those who dedicate themselves to this sacred work, success is certain!

This special bonus is available for a limited time.

Sign up to receive your FREE meditations today!

For those unfamiliar with QR codes, simply open the camera app on your mobile device, hover over the QR code, and tap the link.

Peace and Love,

Kristen Brown